HUMMINGBIRDS
OF COSTA RICA

A male Magenta-throated Woodstar.

HUMMINGBIRDS OF COSTA RICA

Text & Photographs by
Michael & Patricia Fogden

A ZONA TROPICAL PUBLICATION

ISBN 0-970-56782-0

Editors: David Featherstone, Angela Sheehan
Layout design: Michael & Patricia Fogden
Quark design: Zona Creativa, S.A.
Designer: Gabriela Wattson

Published by Distribuidores Zona Tropical, S.A.
S.J.O. 1948
P.O. Box 025216
Miami, FL 33102-5216
www.zonatropical.net

CONTENTS

A male Magenta-throated Woodstar at an orchid, *Stenorrhynchos speciosus*. Note the pollinarium on the hummingbird's bill.

PREFACE

To those who have the happy ability to find adventure among little things, I recommend the hummingbirds. In no other warm-blooded animals, perhaps in no other living creatures of any kind, has nature managed to compress so much beauty, vitality, animation, and complex behavior into so small a compass.

Alexander Skutch (1977)

Of all animated beings . . . the most elegant in form and brilliant in color. The stones and metals polished by art are not comparable to this gem of nature. She has placed it in the order of birds, but among the tiniest of the race . . . she has loaded it with all the gifts of which she has only given other birds a share.

Compte de Buffon (1749)

This book is a celebration of the beauty, vivacity, and extraordinary biology of Costa Rica's hummingbirds. Our interest in these captivating birds began more than twenty years ago, when we came to live in Monteverde. Most mornings we breakfast on our veranda, overlooking a profusion of flowering shrubs that attract many hummers. We augment the nectar supply with feeders containing sugar water that are visited by hundreds of hummingbirds during the day. Sugar water is sometimes said to be bad for hummingbirds and also to make them neglect their role as pollinators of plants. Not so; sugar water is simply a quick energy source that allows them more time to search for insects. It is especially valuable in bad weather, when many flowers are damaged or produce little nectar. On wet, windy days, the feeders are crowded with a multitude of hummers arriving and departing in a steady stream. The feeders are also busy just before dusk, when birds come to top up before going to roost. Nectar is their preferred choice and the hummingbirds do not neglect the flowers around our house. As well as sugar, nectar contains trace amounts of amino acids and vitamins. In spite of the feeders, or perhaps because of them, our flowers get lots of visitors, have a high rate of pollination, and produce abundant fruit. Nor do the feeders affect the timing of the local movements or migrations of our hummingbirds. They continue to arrive and depart at their normal times.

Our interest in hummingbirds has taken us to lovely country throughout Costa Rica. But of all the places where we have watched and photographed them, the most spectacular is our rustic cabin in the Peñas Blancas valley on the Caribbean slope of the Cordillera de Tilarán. It is only 15 km from our home in Monteverde, but getting there involves a mule to carry our gear and a strenuous four- or five-hour trek along narrow precipitous trails that cross several mountain torrents. The scenery is stunning, with incredible vistas of misty ridges receding into the distance. Clumps of flowers grow right up against the deck of our cabin, enabling us to watch hummingbirds at distances down to a few centimeters. Our windows lack glass, so hermits and sicklebills often fly through the cabin, pausing to pick spiders and small insects from the numerous cobwebs. It is our favorite place to photograph hummingbirds.

We have restricted our coverage of Costa Rica's hummingbirds to the species that are resident and breed within the country. According to *A Guide to the Birds of Costa Rica*, by F. Gary Stiles and Alexander F. Skutch, there are forty-five of these, of which we have photographed all but one. The missing species, the Plain-capped Starthroat, is not rare but tends to stay high in trees. We have never encountered one low enough to photograph.

Stiles and Skutch list an additional six hummingbirds that are known from Costa Rica but do not breed there. These include the migrant Ruby-throat, which is a common winter visitor to the dry northwest, and five others that are either of doubtful provenance (mislabeled museum specimens) or vagrants known only from a few old records. Even the most recent of the latter dates back almost fifty years, and most go back more than a century. The Indigo-capped Hummingbird, whose normal range is the Magdalena valley of Colombia, is the most interesting of the "vagrants." Stiles and Skutch say that the only Costa Rican specimen differs too much in various characters to be a Colombian bird; nor does it appear to be an aberrant Steely-vented Hummingbird, nor a hybrid. The specimen was originally given subspecies status by the collector and has even been regarded as a separate species—Alfaro's Hummingbird (*Amazilia alfaroana*). It seems that it was an endemic form that is now extinct.

The scientific classification of hummingbirds is constantly being revised, with many recent changes at the genus and species level, but there has been little agreement in the latest publications on how to treat the more controversial forms. In all matters of taxonomy and nomenclature, therefore, we have again followed *A Guide to the Birds of Costa Rica*, which is widely used, rather than the American Ornithologists' Union's *Checklist of North American Birds* (1998), Volume 5 of the *Handbook of Birds of the World* (1999), or the even more recent *Official List of the Birds of Costa Rica* (2002), published by the Ornithological Association of Costa Rica. We have, however, mentioned alternative names, both Latin and English, in the species accounts. Otherwise, except when discussing taxonomic matters, we have used only English names.

Given the close, mutually beneficial relationship that exists between hummingbirds and flowers, it is not surprising that flowers appear prominently in this book. More than ninety species are illustrated and identified, belonging to thirty-four families and sixty genera. They are listed and indexed on pages 148 and 149. English names are not available for most tropical flowers, so we have had to use Latin names. Our main sources for these are the lists of plants in *Costa Rican Natural History* (The University of Chicago Press, 1983) and *Monteverde: Ecology and Conservation of a Tropical Cloud Forest* (Oxford University Press, 2000), supplemented with identifications made by specialists.

Measurements and weights are given in the metric system. According to the United States Metric Association, this system is now used by every country except the United States, Liberia, and Myanmar. Where possible, we have tried to convey a visual impression of sizes by making comparisons between hummingbirds and other familiar birds.

Anyone writing a book on hummingbirds is deeply indebted to the researchers who have studied and written about their biology. We wish to make particular mention of Crawford Greenewalt, who did so much to elucidate the complexities of feather structure, iridescence, and flight in hummingbirds. He was a pioneer in hummingbird photography. We owe much to the ornithologists who have made Costa Rica a center for hummingbird research. We are particularly grateful to Gary Stiles, Peter Feinsinger, and their associates, for sharing with us their expertise. Their work on hummingbird communities has been invaluable and stimulating. We must also mention Alexander Skutch, who collected life-history information for many of these birds, and Robert Colwell, for his work on hummingbirds and flower mites.

For additional information about hummingbirds, identifications of plants, and other help, we thank John Atwood, Bill Busby, Eladio Cruz, Robert Dean, Luis Gómez, Bill Haber, Barry Hammel, Otto von Helversen, Liz Jones and Abraham Gallo of Rio Tigre Lodge, Alan Masters, Mario Mendez, Francisco Morales, Greg and Kathy Murray, Norman Obando, Dionisio Paniagua, Kurt Ranta and Kori Crane, Marco Saborio, Aaron Sekerak (and staff at La Paz Waterfall Gardens), the Tretti family of Rancho La Ensenada, Andres Vaughan, Roberto Wesson, York Winter, Jim Zook, and Willow Zuchowski. We are grateful to the Organization for Tropical Studies for providing access to facilities and other assistance. Specifically, we thank station directors David and Debbie Clark and Bob Matlock at La Selva, and Luis Gómez at Las Cruces.

We are particularly indebted to Angela Sheehan and David Featherstone for their helpful comments and corrections while editing the manuscript. Also to Stephen Johnson for his expert help with our digital images. Finally, we must thank John McCuen and Marc Roegiers for their enthusiastic support and for allowing us so much freedom in the production of this book.

WHAT IS A HUMMINGBIRD?

Hummingbirds are tiny, confiding, animated, and pugnacious. They include the smallest birds in the world and some that are sublimely beautiful, with glittering, iridescent plumage ornamented with showy tufts and plumes. They have unique flying skills, unmatched by any other birds, and a rare ability to go into torpor. The smallest hummers have the highest metabolic rate of any warm-blooded animal and spend much of their life on a knife-edge, within a few hours of death by starvation. If they were any smaller, they would be unable to produce energy fast enough to survive.

Hummingbirds have tremendous appeal, and their extravagant names give a good idea of the way in which they have captured the imagination. The names are full of allusions to jewels and fairies, good examples being Fiery Topaz, Festive Coquette, Crowned Woodnymph, Sapphire-spangled Emerald, Empress Brilliant, Shining Sunbeam, and Long-tailed Sylph. The ancient Mexican name *huitzitzil* (rays of the sun) is similarly poetic, but modern Latin American names often reflect hummingbird behavior. The Mexican *chuparosa* (rose-sucker) and Brazilian *beija flôr* (flower-kisser) are apt descriptions of their feeding behavior, while the Cuban *zum-zum* is a neat onomatopoeic description of how they sound in flight—much better than the prosaic "hummingbird."

Hummingbirds, which live only in the New World, include about 330 species in more than one hundred genera. They fall into two natural groups that differ in appearance and behavior. About thirty species belong to the subfamily Phaethorninae, or hermits, in which both sexes are clothed in dull brownish plumage. The rest belong to the Trochilinae, or typical hummingbirds, most of which are sexually dimorphic and clad in glittering metallic colors. The majority of hummingbird species are found in the tropics, with diminishing numbers to both north and south. One species breeds as far north as Alaska and another as far south as Tierra del Fuego. Few families of birds have representatives in so many extreme environments, ranging from the humid warmth of equatorial rainforests to the baking heat of deserts and the freezing temperatures of high mountain peaks. They may appear fragile, but hummingbirds are deceptively hardy—the Chimborazo Hillstar and Bearded Helmetcrest survive alongside glaciers at altitudes of 5,000 m in the South American Andes. In Costa Rica, the Volcano Hummingbird thrives above timberline, where frosts are common.

All the most notable attributes of hummingbirds—their size, long slender bill, flying ability, iridescent colors, and social behavior—stem from their dependence on nectar, which they consume while hovering at flowers. The flower connection is the result of a long history of coevolution between hummingbirds and plants. The sugars in nectar are an excellent energy source that can be digested quickly—passage through the birds' intestinal tract can take as little as fifteen minutes. Even so, nectar has one disadvantage. Its high water content means that a hummingbird's crop fills up quickly and then takes about four minutes to empty into the digestive tract. This is why hummingbirds alternate short feeding bouts with a few minutes of sitting around. In total, this waiting time can account for as much as 70 to 80 percent of their day.

Although they depend on flowers for energy, all hummingbirds also need protein, fat, and other nutrients, which they get from eating small insects and other arthropods. Hummingbirds devote much of their time each day to catching insects and do so in two main ways—by hawking for them in flight, often high above the treetops or over water; or by gleaning them from foliage, especially the underside of leaves. Hermits habitually visit spiders' webs, feeding on both the spiders and the small insects caught in the web.

Hummingbirds are renowned for their aggression, not only toward each other, but to other animals, large and small. They attack bees and skipper butterflies that trespass on their flowers, and they relentlessly harass predatory birds as big as eagles—an incongruous sight. Fights between rivals seldom amount to more than chases or buffeting wings, but accidents sometimes happen. We once witnessed a brutal encounter between two male Coppery-headed Emeralds. Even when one combatant was helpless on the ground with a broken wing, the victor continued to attack, jabbing it with its bill.

Although confined to the New World, hummingbirds have long been well-known in the Old World. The English poet John Keats wrote admiringly about them early in the nineteenth century, at about the time when it was fashionable to use hummingbird skins to decorate women's hats. In South America millions were slaughtered for export to Europe. Many of these specimens found their way into museums, and some of the species described from them have never been seen since.

Left a Green Violet-ear hovering below an epiphytic heath, *Satyria meiantha.*

Traditionally, hummingbirds have been thought to share a common ancestor with swifts. This supposed relationship is based on morphological characters, especially the similarity of their wing structure, which differs from that of all other birds. Their arm bones are reduced in length, and the hand bones are lengthened—the wing is almost all "hand." They also have a unique ball-and-socket joint where the shoulder girdle is connected to the very large breast bone. Swifts and hummingbirds share exceptional powers of flight, but experts have long differed as to whether these similarities are due to convergence or to common ancestry. Today, the reality of the relationship is generally accepted, supported by DNA studies and other biochemical evidence. It is now thought that swifts and hummingbirds diverged from their common ancestor as long ago as the beginning of the Tertiary period, sixty-five million years ago.

The traditional division of hummingbirds into two natural groups, hermits and typical hummingbirds, which dates back to John Gould's 1861 classification, is also supported by DNA studies. Relationships within the hermits are straightforward with thirty or so species allocated among five or six genera. But the classification of the three hundred typical hummingbirds is still controversial. Currently more than one hundred hummingbird genera are recognized, half of them monotypic, a sure sign that relationships are poorly understood. With greater understanding, traditional groupings will change and the number of genera will decrease. Progress can be seen in the *Handbook of the Birds of the World*, in which *Rhamphodon* has been transferred to the hermits, the large genus *Amazilia* has been split into four, and ten genera have been merged.

Above Great Dusky Swifts flying to their nests at Iguazú Falls; and **left** a Striped-tailed Hummingbird at *Razisea spicata*, showing ten primaries attached to its long finger bones and six secondaries to the short arm bones.

All hummingbirds are small. Well over a hundred species, perhaps more than 150, weigh 4.5 g or less, making them smaller than any other bird. Even the Giant Hummingbird of the South American Andes, which is nearly twice the size of any other, is hardly bigger than a Barn Swallow. And, with a weight of only 20 g, it is a lot lighter than a House Sparrow. The next-biggest hummingbirds weigh not much more than 12 g, about the same as a Chickadee. They include the Great Sapphirewing, the Sword-billed Hummingbird, and such Costa Rican species as the White-tipped Sicklebill and Violet Sabrewing. The smallest Costa Rican hummer is the male Scintillant Hummingbird, which is 6.5 cm long and weighs just 2 g. It is only fractionally larger than the Cuban Bee Hummingbird, which has the distinction of being the smallest bird in the world. Several Costa Rican species, including the Little Hermit, Fork-tailed Emerald, Snowcap, and Volcano Hummingbird, are not much bigger. More than half of Costa Rica's hummingbirds weigh less than the Black-capped Pygmy-Tyrant, which is the smallest Costa Rican bird in any other family.

Above a male Scintillant Hummingbird at *Rubus rosifolius;* and **right** a Violet Sabrewing at *Aphelandra tridentata.*

Hummingbirds have an extensible tongue, up to twice as long as the bill, with a forked, fringed tip. Early naturalists, finding only insects in the birds' stomachs, thought that hummingbirds caught them in flowers, spearing or entangling them with the tip of their tongue. An alternative idea supposed that the tongue was sticky, like that of an anteater, and that insects stuck to it when it was inserted into flowers. Later, once it was realized that nectar was the real objective, it was thought that the tongue functioned like a drinking straw, in the same way as a butterfly's proboscis.

The way a hummingbird's tongue works remained a source of controversy until at least the 1970s. In fact, hummingbirds lap up nectar rather than suck it through a tube. It is now known that the end of the tongue has two longitudinal channels into which the nectar flows by capillary action. After being carried into the bill, it is squeezed out of the tongue. In real life, the tongue flicks in and out of the flower up to a dozen times a second, bringing a steady flow of nectar.

Note the length of the tongues of the White-tipped Sicklebill **left**, and the female Green-crowned Brilliant **above**, which is feeding from a nectar cup of *Norantea costaricensis*. The latter plant is a strange epiphyte belonging to the Marcgraviaceae, a family characterized by candelabra-like inflorescences. At the base of each flower stalk there is a nectar-secreting cup that is a modified bract.

Unlike flamboyant orioles and tanagers, whose colors are always conspicuous, the iridescence of hummingbirds changes with the viewing angle. It is often fleeting, and even appears black in poor light. The colors of orioles and tanagers are the result of chemical pigments, which absorb some wavelengths of white light and reflect the rest, which the eye sees as the complementary color. By contrast, the iridescent colors of hummingbirds are structural rather than chemical in nature, and are caused by interference. Whether chemical or structural, the colors originate in the feather structure, specifically in the barbules.

Interference can perhaps be understood by considering the familiar rainbow colors seen on a thin film of gasoline on a puddle of water. Light is reflected by both the water and gasoline surfaces but, because of the distance it travels through the thin film of gasoline, light of a particular wavelength reflected by the water is out of phase with light of the same wavelength reflected by the gasoline. The out-of-phase wavelengths interfere with each other and cancel each other out. The remaining wavelengths no longer combine to make white light and are seen as a color. The surface of the gasoline film appears rainbow-colored because the distance light travels through the film, and hence the color produced, varies with the viewing angle. Since the wavelengths of light are very short, interference occurs only with very thin films. In hummingbirds, such films occur in the form of stacks of microscopically thin platelets in the outer layer of the barbules. Further variations in interference effects are caused by minute air bubbles contained within the platelets.

The dazzling iridescence seen on the crown, gorget, and breast of hummingbirds is highly directional, appearing blackish when viewed from the side. It is caused by the mirrorlike surfaces of the color-producing barbules. In the case of the vivid colors of the gorget, the "mirrors" concentrate the color so that it can be seen only from directly in front, as it would be seen by a rival in a head-on confrontation. The flared "ears" of the Green Violet-ear **below left**, and the brilliant gorgets of the Crowned Woodnymph **above left**, and Magenta-throated Woodstar **center left** are good examples. Less brilliant colors result if the "mirrors" are curved so that the iridescence is scattered in all directions. For example, the iridescent greens seen on the body plumage of many hummingbirds, including the Green Violet-ear (**right** visiting *Cavendishia complectens*) are less directional, less intense, and can be seen from almost any angle.

Iridescent colors are rarely found in flight feathers, because the barbules that produce iridescence are modified and twisted in a way that weakens the feather structure. Iridescent flight feathers would not stand up well to the stresses involved in the aerial acrobatics of a hummingbird.

The ability to hover for prolonged periods while feeding at flowers sets hummingbirds apart from all other birds. They, alone among birds, generate lift from both the forward and backward strokes of their wings. Both strokes are made with the wings fully extended, generating maximum lift. In other birds, the backstroke is a recovery stroke, made with partially folded wings, so it generates no lift.

The hummingbird wing differs from that of a "normal" bird in being rigid except at the shoulder joint, which is extremely flexible, allowing free movement in all directions. The wing can rotate about its axis, so that it can change angle by nearly 180 degrees. It is this rotation that allows the hummingbird to invert its wings with each backstroke, enabling the front edge of the wing to lead at all times and so generate lift from both strokes. Smaller changes in wing angle allow the bird to make minute adjustments in its hovering position in all directions. It should not be surprising that the muscles that power the backstroke are much bigger in hummingbirds than in other birds.

The inversion of the wings on the backstroke can be clearly seen in the photographs shown here. For example, the Green Violet-ear **above left** is starting a backstroke. Its wings are inverted, their front edge leads, and the underside of the flight feathers is uppermost.

Because they are articulated only at the shoulder, the wings of hummingbirds function more like those of insects than those of other birds. It is noteworthy, therefore, that the precision flying of hummingbirds is matched or surpassed only by such insects as hoverflies, dragonflies, and hawkmoths.

Above left a Green Violet-ear with wings inverted at the beginning of the backstroke; **below left** a female Purple-throated Mountaingem hovering, with wings at the end of the forward stroke, at a gesneriad, *Gloxinia sylvatica*; and **right** an immature Scintillant Hummingbird with inverted wings at an epiphytic heath, *Vaccinium poasanum*.

As a hummingbird hovers in front of a flower, its rapidly beating wings push it backwards and forwards with each beat. In a big hummingbird with slow wing beats, the jerky movement is clearly visible. In small hummingbirds with wings beating fifty to eighty times per second, the jerkiness is smoothed out. Rapidly beating wings increase the stability of hovering.

Within each species, including hummingbirds, birds flap their wings at a more or less constant rate. This rate follows the same laws that govern the movement of a swinging pendulum, which has a natural frequency that depends on its length. A long pendulum swings more slowly than a short one. In the same way, long wings have a natural flapping frequency that is slower than that of short wings. Birds can and do change the rate at which they flap their wings, perhaps to elude a predator or during a courtship flight, but only for short bursts.

It is commonly supposed that hummingbirds flap their wings faster than other birds. This is generally true, but only because they are smaller than most other birds. When the larger hummingbirds are compared with birds of equal size, hummingbirds are found to have slower wing beats. The Giant Hummingbird flaps its wings only ten times per second, slower than the fourteen times per second of the much bigger mockingbird. Of course, hummingbirds generate twice as much lift per wing beat as other birds, so they can afford to flap more slowly.

Above a Striped-tailed Hummingbird at *Razisea spicata*; and female Purple-throated Mountaingems hovering in front of an epiphytic heath, *Cavendishia melastomoides* **above right**, and an orchid, *Sobralia amabilis* **below right**. Note that two of the hummingbirds have their wings inverted.

The marvellous flying ability of the smaller hummingbirds comes at a high cost, for hovering flight on wings beating fifty to eighty times per second expends an incredible amount of energy. This is on top of an energy expenditure that is already high because of their small size and high body temperature (around 39–42° C). Small, warm bodies lose heat faster than bigger, cool ones.

In fact, tiny hummers like the Scintillant Hummingbird have the highest metabolic rate of any warm-blooded vertebrate, rivaled only by the equally small Pygmy Shrew (*Microsorex hoyi*). To sustain their high metabolic rate, hummingbirds must eat about half their body weight in food a day. Though all hummingbirds eat small insects, it is the calorie-rich nectar that they sip from flowers that fuels their high-energy lifestyle. A reliable supply of nectar, ingested every few minutes, is crucial and it must be digested quickly to make room for more. Nectar, which contains water and calories and not much else, is processed within fifteen to twenty minutes, the waste products emerging as little more than a few crystal-clear droplets **right**.

To cope with long nights, hummingbirds have evolved a remarkable ability. To conserve energy while sleeping, they become torpid and their body temperature drops to near air temperature. They do not necessarily go into torpor every night—it depends on weather conditions and the energy reserves of the individual hummingbird. Torpor is particularly important for small species that live at high altitudes, where frosts and extremely cold nights are the norm. For tiny Scintillant Hummingbirds, some of which live at well over 2,000 m, it is a life-saving ability.

Above left a male Scintillant Hummingbird landing; **below left** a female torpid at night; and **right** a Magenta-throated Woodstar defecating while visiting poinsettia (*Euphorbia pulcherrima*).

Hummingbirds spend a lot of time each day, as much as 70 to 80 percent according to most estimates, sitting around digesting food between feeding bouts. They devote much of this time to preening, scratching and oiling their plumage, keeping it in top-notch condition. Feather maintenance is essential for all birds for efficient insulation and flight, but especially so for such energetic fliers as hummingbirds. Most feather maintenance is done by preening with the bill, although long-billed hummingbirds have a hard time reaching all the parts of their body that need attention. They groom the hard-to-reach places with their feet by scratch-preening. The Sword-billed Hummingbird of South America has a bill so long that it can reach hardly any of its body. To compensate, it has unusually flexible legs and feet, enabling it to scratch even the center of its back, a feat impossible for most hummingbirds. After bouts of preening, hummingbirds often body-shake to fluff and ruffle their plumage, helping it to settle into place.

Hummingbirds are fond of bathing and are often seen dipping into streams and small waterfalls, especially in the late afternoon or at dusk. Sometimes the smaller species bathe in the treetops, taking advantage of wet foliage or the small pools of water that collect in knotholes or the rosettes of bromeliads. Many hummingbirds enjoy bathing in the rain, ruffling their plumage and vibrating their wings ecstatically while spraying droplets of water in all directions.

Above left a Magenta-throated Woodstar preening; **below left** an immature Green-breasted Mango preening; **below right** a Black-crested Coquette ruffling; and **above right** a Purple-throated Mountaingem bathing during a rain shower.

With their lightning reactions and agile flight, adult hummingbirds are a difficult target for most of the usual predators of birds. The Tiny Hawk **right** is reported to ambush male hummingbirds, especially lekking species, while they are singing on their territorial perches. This Tiny Hawk was concealed above a manakin lek. We have also seen Barred Forest-Falcons attempting to ambush hummingbirds at flowers.

Hummingbirds are also preyed upon by snakes, including the Eyelash Viper (*Bothriechis schlegelii*). Of particular interest is a spectacular golden form of this snake (called oropel in Costa Rica, meaning "golden skin"), which lives only in the Caribbean rainforest of Nicaragua and Costa Rica. The oropel is often found in *Heliconia* thickets (**above** in a thicket of *H. imbricata*) coiled on a bright red inflorescence. Although it is alert for any suitable prey, it appears to be intent on catching the hummingbirds that frequent *Heliconia* flowers. It may be that the golden color of the oropel's skin is itself attractive to hummingbirds, for they are inquisitive and always ready to investigate bright patches of color that might signal a new source of nectar. But there is no guarantee of success for the viper. In this case, the viper's fangs struck only the tail of the Rufous-tailed Hummingbird.

Because of their size, the tiniest hummingbirds are also vulnerable to a wide variety of predators that usually subsist on large insects. There are records of hummingbirds being eaten by frogs, by leaping fish, and by praying mantises. And instances of their being caught in the huge orb webs of *Nephila* spiders are quite common.

HUMMINGBIRDS AND FLOWERS

Most tropical plants enlist the help of animals for pollen dispersal. The most important pollinators are bees, but there are many others, including other insects, hummingbirds, and bats. Since flowers "want" to be pollinated, they have features that match the physical and sensory abilities of pollinators. To achieve pollination, flowers provide a reward, advertise it, and are so constructed that visitors come into contact with their stamens and stigma.

The commonest reward is nectar but others include pollen and less usual substances, such as waxes, oils, and perfumes (the latter used by orchid bees as sexual pheromones). Nectar varies in the sugars it contains. Flowers pollinated by hummingbirds, butterflies, hawkmoths, and many bees secrete nectar that is rich in sucrose, whereas those pollinated by bats and by passerine birds (including American orioles and tanagers, Australian honeyeaters, and Old World sunbirds) have nectar rich in glucose and fructose, sugars that are also found in fruits. The significance of these intriguing differences is unknown, but they do not seem to matter much to hummingbirds and bats. Hummingbirds happily feed on leftover nectar in bat flowers, while bats routinely empty our hummingbird feeders full of sucrose solution.

Flowers have evolved a variety of adaptations to attract specific pollinators. Hummingbird flowers are diurnal, brightly colored, odorless (birds do not have much of a sense of smell), and tubular (to fit a hummingbird's bill). Hawkmoth flowers are nocturnal, white (to show up in the dark), fragrant, and also tubular (to fit a moth's proboscis). Bat flowers are nocturnal and usually pale, with a strong musky odor. Some have "sonar guides," which bats detect by echolocation. Flowers pollinated by passerine birds, bees, and butterflies, which settle to feed, provide perches or landing sites, whereas those pollinated by animals that hover to feed, including hummingbirds, hawkmoths, and many bats, are free of obstructions.

Some flowers have mixed adaptations that attract more than one type of pollinator. They may be hedging their bets, or they may be in the process of changing from relying on one type of pollinator to another. *Gonzalagunia rosea* (page 140), with its fragrant, pinkish flowers with a short tubular corolla, attracts bees, butterflies, and hummingbirds, all of which may be effective pollinators. The powder-puff blossoms of *Inga* trees (pages 34, 113, and 116) are puzzling. Most appear to be pollinated by hawkmoths, but they also attract hummingbirds, bats, and a variety of insects. *Inga vera* flowers open an hour or two before dusk and secrete abundant nectar, which is taken avidly by hummingbirds, but they do not appear to release pollen until after dark, so they cannot be pollinated until then. The attractiveness of *Inga oerstediana* varies from tree to tree. Some individuals are "hummingbird trees" that attract hummers throughout the day, others attract none at all. Ironically, it is possible to see more hummingbirds at *Inga oerstediana* than at typical hummingbird flowers. At one we saw twelve species in less than an hour, and twenty over the course of three or four days.

Hummingbird flowers are commonly red, a color that contrasts with green foliage and probably restricts visits by those insects that cannot see red. There are two main types. One sort has long, tubular flowers (mostly 30–40 mm long) that secrete copious nectar. They tend to be scattered and visited by "traplining" hummingbirds (pages 44 and 45). The other has short, tubular flowers (mostly less than 20 mm long). These have less nectar, but are massed together in numbers big enough to be worth defending by territorial hummingbirds (pages 48 and 49). There are consequences for the plants. Trapliners tend to carry pollen from plant to plant, which results in cross-pollination and enhanced reproductive success. Territorial hummingbirds foster self-pollination. Sometimes they visit so many flowers on the same plant that their face gets covered with white or golden pollen, making them look like a different species. Hummingbirds that intrude into territories to steal nectar are probably more useful to a plant than the territorial owner. Since intruders visit flowers only briefly before being chased off, they perhaps deliver pollen to a plant of the same species some distance away.

One other point to be considered is why some flowers use hummingbirds as pollinators rather than insects. After all, insects can be attracted with a smaller reward of nectar. The probable reason is that hummingbirds are more reliable as pollinators when the weather is bad, particularly at high altitudes. Bees and butterflies are not active when it is too wet or too cold, so flowers dependent on them fail to be pollinated. Hummingbirds are active in all kinds of weather, so it is no surprise that there are many more hummingbird-pollinated plants in the highlands than the lowlands.

Left a Green Violet-ear at an epiphytic bromeliad, *Tillandsia multicaulis.*

Certain plant families are particularly important for hummingbirds. A glance at the list of flowers that appear in this book (pages 148 and 149) shows that some of the most notable are the Heliconiaceae, Bromeliaceae, Ericaceae, Rubiaceae, Acanthaceae, and Gesneriaceae families. These flowers are ornithophilous, or bird-loving, and exhibit various adaptations for pollination by hummingbirds.

Most hummingbird flowers are either red themselves, or have red bracts or leaves that advertise or flag their presence, red being a color that is conspicuous to hummers but not to most insect competitors. The three flowers illustrated here are good examples. The ginger has yellow or reddish flowers embedded between overlapping red bracts; the heath has red flowers surrounded by red leaves; and hotlips has white flowers that contrast with two large red bracts.

Though hummingbirds often visit flowers of other colors, there is little doubt that they prefer red. Go for a walk in the forest wearing articles of red clothing, and hummingbirds will fly right up to you to investigate. Other colors do not provoke the same behavior.

The flowers shown here also conform to the hummingbird type in other ways. All three have a tubelike corolla that fits the slender bill of a hummingbird, and have little or no scent (which might attract insects). Two of them lack a landing platform that would provide easy access for insects. Hotlips is an exception in this respect, because its large red bracts provide a landing platform that is used by various butterflies.

Above a Green-crowned Brilliant at a ginger, *Costus wilsonii*; **above right** a Green Violet-ear at an epiphytic heath, *Gonocalyx costaricensis*; and **below right** a Coppery-headed Emerald at hotlips (*Cephaelis elata*).

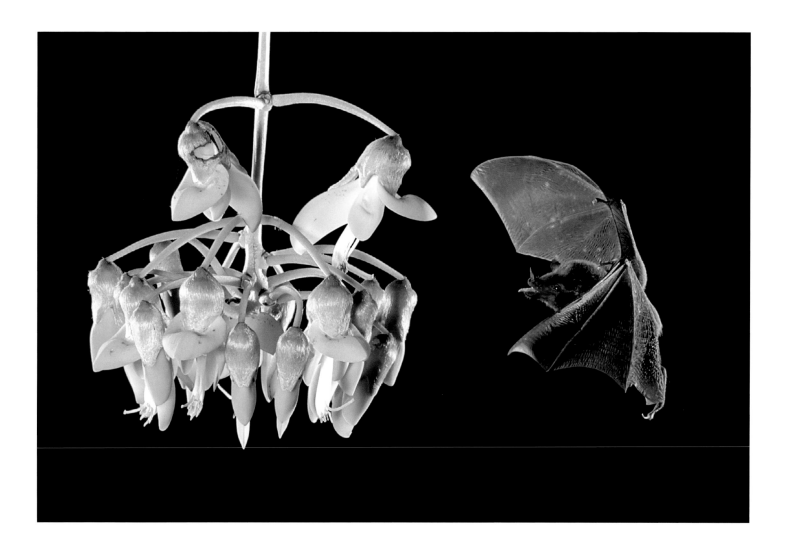

Bat flowers open at night and produce copious nectar, some of which is still left in the morning. It is this excess nectar that makes bat flowers appealing to hummingbirds—for an hour or two after dawn, they often attract frantic activity. The amount of nectar can be significant. Gary Stiles found that the breeding season of Green-crowned Brilliants in his study area in Braulio Carillo National Park was timed to coincide with the flowering of three species of bat-pollinated *Marcgravia*, rather than with typical hummingbird flowers.

We have watched hummingbirds at a variety of classic bat flowers. The most popular in our experience is a bromeliad, *Vriesia nephrolepis*, that is abundant around our house and regularly attracts six species. The hummingbirds are probably doing no more than finishing up excess nectar left by bats from the previous night, but it is possible that they sometimes act as pollinators. They certainly come into contact with the stamens and stigmas, but whether or not the flowers are still receptive in the morning is not clear.

Although most bat flowers open after dark, they often begin secreting nectar before they open. Some hummingbirds take advantage of this. Just before dusk, they visit *Norantea* (pages 15 and 90) and *Marcgravia* inflorescences, which secrete nectar in open "cups" or "flasks" separate from the flowers. Some Violet Sabrewings are even more enterprising. They have learned to visit the flowers of the bromeliad *Vriesia nephrolepis* in the late evening to pierce and extract nectar from buds that are still closed.

Above left a Geoffroy's Long-tongued Bat and **below left** a female Green-crowned Brilliant at a bromeliad, *Vriesia nephrolepis*; and **above** an Underwood's Long-tongued Bat at *Mucuna urens*.

Two types of nocturnal flowers are visited by moths. One type provides a landing platform for moths that settle to feed. The other is visited by hawkmoths, which hover to feed. Hawkmoths are more or less the nocturnal counterparts of hummingbirds. They have similar hovering skills and a long proboscis with which they probe long tubular flowers. In fact, hawkmoths have tongues ranging up to 25 cm long, more than double the length of a Sword-billed Hummingbird's bill.

Clusia stenophylla is an example of a flower that is pollinated by moths that settle. For an hour or two after daybreak, it also attracts hummingbirds, which mop up any excess nectar. A number of fragrant white flowers also attract moths at night and hummingbirds throughout the day, not just at dawn. *Quararibea costaricensis*, a common cloud forest tree, is a good example. It has typical moth flowers, with a sweet fragrance, that hawkmoths visit and presumably pollinate at night. By day, the flowers attract hummingbirds.

The brushlike blossoms of *Inga* trees (see also pages 113 and 116) provide other examples. In the Monteverde area, *Inga oerstediana* attracts at least twenty species of hummingbird, and *I. sierrae* at least a dozen.

It is not clear to what extent hummingbirds pollinate these flowers. It may be that they are receptive only at night, but those that secrete nectar all day may well be receptive during daylight hours. The trees may in effect be relying mostly on moths but taking advantage of hummingbirds when the weather is too cold or too wet for moths to be active.

Above a female Magenta-throated Woodstar at *Inga sierrae*; and Coppery-headed Emeralds at *Quararibea costaricensis* **above right**, and *Clusia stenophylla* **below right**.

Bees are enormously important as pollinators and visit a prodigious variety of flowers. Although they favor blue, purple, and ultra-violet (and see poorly at the red end of the spectrum), bees visit flowers of almost any color. Some visit hummingbird flowers for their copious nectar, stealing it through holes bitten into the back of the flower. Hummingbirds reciprocate and take nectar from many bee flowers. *Passiflora edulis*, being visited by a Striped-tailed Hummingbird **above**, is one of many passion flowers that are pollinated by bees.

Bee flowers are especially important for hummingbirds in the dry forests of Guanacaste, where specialized hummingbird flowers are few and far between. Hummingbirds there breed in the dry season, coinciding with the mass flowering of many bee-pollinated trees, particularly legumes. Other bee-pollinated trees which are important to hummingbirds include the highly synchronized, mass-flowering "big bang" species, *Tabebuia ochracea* and *T. impetiginosa* (pages 95 and 112).

Butterfly flowers secrete moderate quantities of nectar, often in a long, thin spur that fits the proboscis of butterflies. The flowers are often red or contrasting patterns of red, orange, and yellow. Like hummingbirds, many butterflies can see red, and butterfly flowers inevitably attract the attention of hummingbirds. The amount of nectar these flowers produce is too small to keep the larger species interested, but sufficient for many small hummers. The widespread balsam *Impatiens walleriana*, which comes in various shades of red or pink, is a good example of a butterfly flower. Scintillant Hummingbirds **above left** are sporadic visitors, as are at least a dozen other small hummingbirds, including Little Hermits and female mountaingems. The red and yellow flowers of the milkweed *Asclepias curassavica* **below left** are also visited by both hummingbirds and butterflies. In this case, the visitor is an ithomiine, *Mechanitis lysimnia*.

Many exotic garden flowers that flourish in Costa Rica are popular with hummingbirds. Some of these are from elsewhere in Central and South America and are adapted for pollination by hummers, so it is no surprise that they are visited by Costa Rican species. Good examples include *Sanchezia nobilis* from Ecuador **above**, here being visited by a Rufous-tailed Hummingbird, and the mint *Salvia involucrata* from Mexico **left**, here being visited by a Green Violet-ear. These plants are only exotic in the Costa Rican context, for they and the hummers occur together naturally in Ecuador and Mexico.

Other exotic flowers visited by hummingbirds are from further afield. The bottlebrush tree (*Callistemon violaceum*) being visited by a Rufous-tail **below right** is from Australia, where it would normally be pollinated by honeyeaters, while the *Aloe* providing nectar to a Green-crowned Brilliant **above right** is from Africa, where it would be visited naturally by

sunbirds. Because they are adapted to be pollinated by birds, flowers like the bottlebrush and *Aloe* share many of the characteristics of hummingbird flowers. It is not surprising that they are attractive to hummingbirds.

The popularity of *Stachytarpheta frantzii* is a little surprising. Though it occurs naturally in Guanacaste, this verbenaceous shrub is commonly seen as an ornamental in gardens all over Costa Rica. With its numerous purple florets, it looks like an insect flower and indeed attracts a multitude of bees and many butterflies, especially skippers. Nevertheless, it is extraordinarily attractive to hummingbirds, and we have records of it being visited by thirty species, including coquettes, thorntails, and other species typical of the forest canopy. Since it attracts canopy hummers down to shrub level, it is a great boon to birders. Its numerous appearances in the photographs in this book (pages 53, 69, 99, 101, 102, 108, and 114) testify to its popularity.

FEEDING STRATEGIES

As many as sixteen or seventeen different hummingbirds occur together in parts of Costa Rica, each of them occupying a slightly different niche. The ways in which they are segregated depend partly on their structure, especially of their bill, and partly on their behavior.

It is often said that the length and curvature of the bills of hummingbirds fit the flowers at which they feed. This is true in a general way, but there is seldom a simple one-to-one relationship. On the contrary, most hummingbird flowers are visited by many different species. Based on their bills, hummingbirds are best divided into only two major groups, one consisting of hummingbirds with a long, often curved bill, and a much bigger group with a relatively short, straight bill.

All the hummingbirds in the first group, which includes the hermits, Lancebill, Violet Sabrewing, Magnificent Hummingbird, and others, visit specialized flowers with a long tubular corolla. There is an enormous overlap in the selection of flowers that they visit. In the Costa Rican lowlands, for example, any flowers of *Heliconia pogonantha* or *H. longa* are likely to be visited by all the hermits in the area.

The only hermit that depends on a limited selection of flowers is the White-tipped Sicklebill. Its extraordinary bill matches the strongly curved corolla of *Centropogon granulosus*, and a few species of *Heliconia*, but is too acutely curved to be inserted easily into any other flowers. Even though the Sicklebill is locked into this relationship, the reverse is not true. Other hermits visit all the flowers used by the Sicklebill. Their bills may not fit the flowers so perfectly, but their long, flexible tongues easily compensate.

The second group of hummingbirds, which have relatively short bills, are capable of feeding at virtually any flower with a short corolla. A clump of the rubiaceous shrub *Hamelia patens* in the Caribbean lowlands may well attract six or seven short-billed species on most mornings and many more over a period of days or weeks. Even so, there is a tendency for the hummingbirds with the shortest bills to visit the shortest flowers, and those with longer bills to use longer flowers. For example, the Coppery-headed Emerald, with a bill 14 mm long, and the Purple-throated Mountaingem, with a bill 19 mm long, are two cloud forest hummers that visit many epiphytic heaths. In the Monteverde cloud forest, Emeralds favor two species that have corollas less than 16 mm long, and rarely visit four others, with corollas more than 18 mm long, which are preferred by Mountaingems.

Hummingbirds are also segregated by behavior. Peter Feinsinger and Robert Colson, both of whom studied hummingbirds in Costa Rica, classified hummingbirds according to the ways in which they visit and exploit flowers—in other words, according to their ecological roles or "professions." Their category of "high-reward trapliners" corresponds to the long-billed hummingbirds, described above, that trapline specialized flowers with a long corolla. Their "territorialists" defend large patches of flowers against all other hummingbirds, including members of their own species.

In addition to trapliners and territorialists, they mention such antisocial professions as marauders, filchers, and piercers, all of which engage in stealing nectar. Marauders and filchers steal from territorial hummingbirds, while piercers extract nectar through holes that they make in the base of flowers.

These ecological roles are useful shorthand for hummingbird behavior, but they should not be considered as rigid categories. A typical territorialist does not necessarily defend a territory at all times, and even a hermit defends flowers occasionally. The way a hummingbird forages is determined by opportunity and necessity, and it adjusts its behavior accordingly, from season to season, day to day, or even hour to hour. A hummingbird may be a territorialist first thing in the morning, when nectar is flowing strongly in the flowers it is defending, then trapline intermittently when the flow decreases. A filcher that steals from a territorialist in the morning is a low-reward trapliner when it feeds at the same flowers, now undefended, in the afternoon. Or it may even become a territorialist by defending the flowers against other small hummers. Many species are occasional piercers.

Left a Purple-throated Mountaingem at an epiphytic heath, *Cavendishia bracteata*.

Long-billed and short-billed hummingbirds usually feed at flowers that match the length and shape of their bill. The Green Hermit feeding at *Centropogon granulosus* **above**, and the Coppery-headed Emerald visiting an epiphytic heath, *Cavendishia capitulata* **below right**, are excellent examples. Nevertheless, the differences between the two groups in feeding behavior and flower choice are not absolute. Long-billed hummingbirds can and often do visit short flowers. Judging by the amount of pollen on its bill, the Long-tailed Hermit feeding at the short flowers of *Heliconia imbricata* **left** has been doing so for some while. Hummingbirds with a short bill occasionally extract nectar from long flowers by using their tongue, which is up to twice as long as their bill. We have even seen Rufous-tailed Hummingbirds systematically feeding at the long, strongly curved flowers of *Heliconia pogonantha* and *H. stilesii*, plants more typically visited by White-tipped Sicklebills. The Green Violet-ear

feeding at the long flowers of *Ravnia triflora* **above** is another example.

The choices hummingbirds make are decided by efficiency and competition. It can be awkward for a long-billed hummingbird to maneuver rapidly among many small flowers, and it takes much longer for a short-billed hummer to imbibe nectar if its tongue has to be extruded several times as far as usual. Normally it is more efficient for hummingbirds to choose flowers that fit their bills. However, if the "right" flowers are scarce, or the "wrong" flowers are abundant and undefended, the opposite choice may make better sense.

"Traplining" is a term borrowed from fur trappers who traditionally set traps in long lines and checked them periodically. Traplining hummingbirds have long bills, often curved, and feed at tubular flowers that are too long for hummingbirds with shorter bills. These flowers produce copious nectar (hence the high-reward), but they are too scattered to be worth defending. Trapliners exploit them by tracing a long route through the forest, visiting as many flowers as possible, and retracing the route several times a day. Hermits are the classic high-reward trapliners. The Green Hermit fills the role in the Costa Rican cloud forest, the Sicklebill and other hermits in the lowlands. There are no hermits above 2,000 m, so there is a vacancy there for a high-altitude trapliner. It is filled by the Magnificent Hummingbird, particularly the female, which has a longer bill than the male.

High-reward trapliners visit many different species of flowers in the course of their rounds, which increases the risk that pollen will be mixed up and transported to the wrong flowers. High-reward flowers are consequently constructed so that their stamens and stigmas come into contact with a specific part of a hummingbird's body as it feeds. They come into contact with the bill in some species, the crown or throat in others. This helps to ensure that pollination is effective and minimizes the possibility of hybridization. The Bronzy Hermit seen **above right** is carrying two patches of pollen, one on the crown of its head from the passion flower that it is visiting, and another on its bill from some other flower.

Above left a White-tipped Sicklebill at *Heliconia reticulata*; **below left** a Long-tailed Hermit at *Heliconia pogonantha*; **above right** a Bronzy Hermit at a passion flower, *Passiflora vitifolia*; and **below right** a female Magnificent Hummingbird at *Centropogon gutierrezii*.

Low-reward trapliners tend to be small or very small with short to medium-length bills. They are at the bottom of the hummingbird pecking order and forage at a mixture of mainly small flowers that are not being defended by more dominant species. These flowers may be in patches that are too small to be worth defending, too scattered, or too low in quality. Good examples of low-reward trapliners include the Fork-tailed Emerald, female mountaingems, and female Coppery-headed and White-tailed Emeralds. A few are quite large. The Green Violet-ear, for example, is as big as most territorialists but often traplines and seldom defends a territory.

Most hummingbirds behave as low-reward trapliners at least part of the time. Even aggressive territorialists such as male Rufous-tailed and Steely-vented Hummingbirds trapline when flowers are scarce. And they routinely do so in the late morning or afternoon, when the flow of nectar has declined in the flowers they defended earlier in the day.

Most low-reward trapliners visit many flowers that are typically pollinated by insects. In fact, the Volcano and Scintillant Hummingbirds are so small, and visit insect flowers so frequently, that they could be regarded as "honorary insects."

Above left a female Purple-throated Mountaingem at an orchid, *Elleanthus hymenophorus*; **left** a Fork-tailed Emerald at a gesneriad, *Kohleria spicata*; and **right** a female Volcano Hummingbird at a climbing lily, *Bomarea hirsuta*.

The most aggressive, dominant territorialists tend to be medium-sized hummingbirds weighing between 4.5 and 5.5 g. Species such as the Fiery-throated and Rufous-tailed Hummingbirds, and male mountaingems, are good examples. Bigger species tend to be marauders and take what they want without wasting effort on territorial defense, while most smaller hummers are would-be territorialists, but rarely find a patch of flowers to defend. However, given the opportunity, even tiny Scintillant Hummers defend flowers against other Scintillants.

Territorialists have a relatively short, straight bill and feed at flowers with a short corolla. They set up territories wherever sufficient flowers for their needs are concentrated in an area small enough to be defended. They are very aggressive, spending much of their time chasing off intruders.

Having a good territory ensures that a reliable supply of nectar is available at all times, which helps the birds to stay in excellent condition. A good territory also attracts females looking for a mate. The most important function of a hummingbird's dazzling plumage is for territorial defense, and the reason that the full splendor of the crown and gorget can be appreciated only from directly in front is that this is the way rivals see it in face-to-face conflict. Because of their brighter plumage, it is mainly male hummingbirds that are territorialists. Most females are smaller, duller, and lack the head-on ornamentation of males. They have little success defending a territory and generally forage in some other way. There are exceptions. Female Fiery-throated, Cinnamon, and Steely-vented Hummingbirds, among others, are as brightly colored as the males, and they too defend territories.

Above a male Purple-throated Mountaingem at a mistletoe, *Psittacanthus ramiflorus*; **above right** a Rufous-tailed Hummingbird at *Hamelia patens*; and **below right** a Fiery-throated Hummingbird at *Fuchsia microphylla*.

Typically, marauders are only a little bigger than territorialists. They are medium to large hummingbirds (weighing about 6.5 to 9 g) that barge into a territory and help themselves to whatever they want, simply ignoring the frenzied efforts of the owners to eject them. They are big enough and aggressive enough to defend a territory of their own, but seldom do so. The reason is quite simple. Defending a territory is expensive in energy, so why bother when you can get what you want with less effort.

Regular marauders include the Green-breasted Mango, the White-necked Jacobin, and, to a lesser extent, the Brown Violet-ear. Most other large hummers, including the Violet Sabrewing, Scaly-breasted Hummingbird, and Red-footed Plumeleteer, are occasional marauders, but all of these spend more time foraging as trapliners or territorialists.

Strictly speaking, a hummingbird does not have to be big to be a marauder. A tiny Coppery-headed Emerald becomes a marauder whenever it intrudes into a meager patch of insect flowers defended by an even tinier Scintillant Hummer. It is just a question of relative size, though small hummingbirds obviously have fewer opportunities to be marauders than bigger species.

Above a Green-breasted Mango at *Heliconia latispatha*; **above right** a White-necked Jacobin at *Palicourea guianensis*; and **below right** a Brown Violet-ear at hotlips (*Cephaelis elata*).

Filchers are small hummingbirds that sneak around the edges of territories and steal nectar when the territory owner is not looking, usually when it is busy chasing some other intruder. Often they are very persistent, retreating into dense cover when they are chased, only to return again and again. Scintillant Hummingbirds are particularly adept at avoiding pursuit by dodging in and out of foliage.

Many low-reward trapliners double as filchers, good examples being the Fork-tailed Emerald, both coquettes, and tiny Volcano and Scintillant Hummers. Perhaps the most adept filcher is the Magenta-throated Woodstar, which often looks and sounds like a huge bee. Its rapidly beating wings produce a loud buzz that is more bumblebee-like than the softer hum of other small hummers. Its flight, too, is characteristically smooth and insect-like, quite unlike that of other Costa Rican hummingbirds. The resemblance to a bee is close enough to deceive territorial hummingbirds at least for a while, for Woodstars remain undetected longer than other filchers.

Above a Magenta-throated Woodstar at an epiphytic heath, *Cavendishia capitulata*; **above right** a female Volcano Hummingbird at *Fuchsia paniculata*; and **below right** a female Black-crested Coquette at *Stachytarpheta frantzii*.

Piercers practice a different type of theft, stealing nectar from hermits and other high-reward trapliners. Their bills are too short to reach the nectar bonanza at the bottom of the long flowers visited and pollinated by hermits, so they gain access to the nectary by piercing the base of the flower. This is unhelpful to the flower (as well as to the next hermit to come along) because piercers never come into contact with the stamens or stigma of the flowers, and so never pollinate them.

The Striped-tailed Hummingbird is the most persistent piercer among highland hummingbirds, while the Purple-crowned Fairy fills a similar role in the lowlands. However, one of them is more incorrigible than the other. The Striped-tail has a typical hummingbird bill and visits many flowers legitimately from the front (page 119) and pollinates them. The Fairy, on the other hand, has a short, sharply pointed bill that it uses to pierce just about every flower it visits. It is a habitual nectar thief and seldom if ever pollinates anything.

While the Fairy and Striped-tail are the only Costa Rican hummingbirds that might be termed "professional piercers," there are many others that practice piercing to some extent. Two of the hermits—the Band-tailed Barbthroat and the Little Hermit—do so frequently. Other species that we have seen piercing include the Violet Sabrewing, Fork-tailed Emerald, Fiery-throated Hummer, Rufous-tailed Hummer, and Purple-throated Mountaingem.

Many hummingbirds have learned to take nectar through the holes chewed by bees into the back of flowers. For them, it is probably just a short step from this behavior to making holes themselves.

Above a Purple-crowned Fairy piercing a flower of *Heliconia hirsuta;* and **right** a Striped-tailed Hummingbird piercing *Poikilacanthus macranthus.*

Hummingbirds have many avian competitors. One of the most important is the Slaty Flowerpiercer, a highland species that uses its hooked bill to pierce the nectaries of flowers and steal the contents. Here **above right** a Flowerpiercer is piercing a sleeping hibiscus, *Malvaviscus palmanus.* Some short-billed hummingbirds take the opportunity to feed through the holes made by Flowerpiercers.

Hummingbirds must also compete with insects. Even though hummingbird flowers and insect flowers differ in so many respects, they still get visits from the "wrong" nectar feeders. Bees, including stingless species such as *Trigona* **left**, often steal nectar by chewing holes into the nectaries of hummingbird flowers, in this case the passion flower *Passiflora vitifolia.* Again, some hummingbirds take advantage of this. Here **above** a Stripe-tailed Hummingbird is

feeding at a hole in a lily, *Bomarea caldasii*, made by a bumblebee (*Bombus*).

Other competitors are less obvious but more interesting. Flower mites (*Rhinoseius*) live inside flowers, where they feed on nectar and pollen. As well as competing for food, they take advantage of hummingbirds by hitching a ride between flowers. The mites jump onto a hummingbird's bill as it feeds and race up it to shelter in the bird's nostrils. Different mites are specific to different flowers, so more than one species may hitch a ride at the same time. Each mite has to identify the correct flower at which to disembark and has only a second or two in which to make the decision and hasten down the bill. These mites **right** are disembarking from a Long-tailed Hermit visiting a passion flower, *Passiflora vitifolia*. For their size, flower mites are said to run about as fast as a cheetah!

THE HUMMINGBIRD'S YEAR

The annual cycle of all birds includes activities that demand time, energy, and other resources beyond those required for daily maintenance. Breeding is the most critical. It requires enormously increased energy expenditure for courtship, nest building, egg production, and feeding young. Molt is less challenging, but it still involves an increase in metabolic rate of about 30 percent. Molt follows immediately after breeding, and both activities take place when food and other resources are plentiful. Birds that migrate long distances face further demands in order to accumulate migratory fat, although this is not a factor for Costa Rican hummingbirds (apart from the Ruby-throat), whose seasonal movements are relatively short.

Hummingbirds are polygamous, and all nesting activities are carried out by the female unaided. As far as males are concerned, breeding begins and ends with courtship and mating, and many spend an inordinate amount of time advertising their services. How males attract females mostly depends on their ability, or lack if it, to defend a territory containing a rich source of nectar.

Male Fiery-throated Hummingbirds, mountaingems, and most other dominant territorialists establish their desirability as a mate by the quality of the flowers in their territory. The better the flowers, the more likely they are to be chosen by females. Male Fiery-throated Hummers are known to defend more flowers than they need and allow females to use the surplus.

In many species, males establish their status by direct competition. In some Costa Rican hummers (fifteen at least), males join singing assemblies (leks) which range in size from as few as two or three birds to twenty or more in the Long-tailed Hermit. Leks of this species can be in excess of a hundred in South America. Most lekking males have squeaky, monotonous songs that they repeat interminably for much of the year. Within an assembly, males defend several perches and compete for central positions because females prefer to mate with the central males. For the most part, hummingbird species that perform in singing assemblies are nonterritorial for one reason or another. Hermits, for example, trapline widely dispersed flowers that are not defendable, while many small hummers are too subordinate to defend patches of rich flowers.

Several small hummingbirds advertise in a different way. They live in open country, or high in the canopy, and have spectacular aerial displays, often accompanied by sound effects made by the wings. Costa Rican examples include the Magenta-throated Woodstar, Volcano and Scintillant Hummingbirds, and probably the Green Thorntail and Coquettes.

The nesting and molting seasons of Costa Rican birds typically run from March or April to about October or November. The seasonality of hummingbirds is more variable, since it depends on the availability of preferred flowers. In lowland areas, hummingbirds nest mainly in the dry season, from December or January to May or June, when nectar-rich hummingbird flowers are most abundant. Timing is similar in the dry forest, where specialized hummingbird flowers are scarce and seasonality revolves around bee flowers. In Monteverde and other highland areas, cloud forest hummingbirds begin nesting toward the end of the year, when the weather is often unpleasantly cold and wet. It is the time when the colorful epiphytic heaths they prefer are flowering most profusely.

The majority of Costa Rican hummingbirds make short seasonal migrations from areas where flowers are declining to more favorable areas. Altitudinal movements are common as hummers shift up and down mountainsides in response to seasonal and local variations in the abundance of flowers. On the Caribbean slope of the Cordillera de Tilarán, the leguminous tree *Inga oerstediana* flowers profusely in May and June and is a magnet for numerous species—Brown Violet-ears and Jacobins move up from lower altitudes and Coppery-headed Emeralds and Brilliants move down from above, while some Steely-vented Hummers cross the divide from the Pacific slope.

The Ruby-throat is the only Costa Rican hummingbird to make a long migration. It travels up to 4,000 km from the eastern United States to Central America. Many individuals fly nonstop for 800 km across the Gulf of Mexico, while others go around. It is a notable achievement for so small a bird, though no more remarkable than the flights of numerous Old World migrants. Some Willow Warblers (which are about the size of Tennessee Warblers) migrate a prodigious 12,000 km between their breeding grounds in northern Eurasia and wintering grounds in sub-Saharan Africa. Their journey includes flying nonstop for several thousand kilometers across the Mediterranean Sea and Sahara Desert.

Left a female Green Hermit feeding her young.

Hermits' nests are different from those of typical hummingbirds and very distinctive. They are almost invariably attached to the underside of the tip of a drooping palm frond or *Heliconia* leaf, low in the forest undergrowth. The supporting leaf, arching overhead, provides a waterproof shelter and partial protection from the prying eyes of predators. When she begins to construct the nest, the female hermit has to work on the wing, using cobwebs to attach fragments of plant material to the drooping leaf. Every so often she circles the leaf, facing inward, delicately winding strands of spider silk round and round the growing nest, binding it securely to its flimsy support. The finished nest is shaped like an inverted cone and usually has a long straggling tail of dead leaves.

When sitting on the nest incubating her eggs or brooding small chicks, a female hermit always faces inward, her head and neck forced backwards into what appears to be an excruciatingly uncomfortable position. It is also noteworthy that she hovers to feed her chicks, rather than perching on the rim of the nest.

As in other hummingbirds, male hermits generally consort with the female only long enough to fertilize the eggs, and take no part in building the nest, incubating the eggs, or feeding the young. However, a degree of minimal cooperation has been found in two species. Over the course of four years, Alexander Skutch watched a male Bronzy Hermit that occasionally sat in a female's nest and guarded it against intrusions by other hummingbirds. Similar behaviour has been observed in the Band-tailed Barbthroat.

Left a female Little Hermit incubating; and **right** a male Band-tailed Barbthroat attending a female while she builds her nest.

The nests of typical hummingbirds (except for a few South American species that nest in caves) are rather similar in construction and appearance and easily recognized. Each tiny structure is a dainty cup saddled on a twig or branch, constructed from green moss, plant fibers, fern scales, downy seeds, and other soft materials, all bound together with cobwebs. Nests are often characteristically ornamented. Many hummingbirds that build in the forest understory, like the Crowned Woodnymph, Violet-headed Hummer, and Striped-tailed Hummer, drape their nests with strands of moss. Those that nest in sunny positions, like the Rufous-tailed Hummingbird, often use lichens. The end result is almost always a well-camouflaged structure that is both exquisite and practical.

All hummingbirds lay two tiny, elongated, white eggs that are incubated by the female for fourteen to nineteen days. At most hummingbird nests that we have watched, the female has returned as regularly as clockwork to feed her nestlings,

every twenty-five to thirty minutes or so, bringing them a mixture of nectar and tiny insects. She feeds them by regurgitation, thrusting her rapier-like bill deep into their throats—an unnerving sight. The chicks stay in the nest for eighteen to twenty-eight days, depending on the prevailing weather and availability of flowers. By the time they are ready to leave, the chicks completely fill the nest.

Sadly, many nestlings never fledge, for hummingbirds' nests fail just as frequently as those of other tropical birds, plundered by toucans, jays, squirrels, snakes, and a host of other predators.

Above left a female Violet-headed Hummingbird incubating; **above right** (this page) a female Striped-tailed Hummingbird feeding her young; **opposite above** a female Rufous-tailed Hummingbird incubating; and **opposite below** well-feathered White-necked Jacobin nestlings.

Feathers deteriorate with age, so all birds have to replace their plumage every year to ensure that it functions efficiently. Molting requires additional energy and nutrients and at the same time reduces performance. It is a costly event in the annual cycle of birds. In most, including hummingbirds, it follows immediately after breeding, the two activities being squeezed into a time of year when plenty of food is available.

Hummingbirds undergo one complete molt a year, lasting four to five months. Flight and contour feathers molt at the same time, the renewal of the all-important primary feathers usually spanning the whole period. Primary molt begins with the short, innermost primary and proceeds outward. The Snowcap (**below left** visiting *Warszewiczia coccinea*) has undergone a drastic beginning to its molt. Its five innermost primaries have been shed and are in various stages of growth, while five old, faded primaries remain.

Hummingbirds are unique among birds in reversing the sequence of molt of their two outermost primaries, an adaptation that preserves the aerodynamic efficiency of the wing tip. This reversal can be seen in the Green Violet-ear (**above** visiting an orchid, *Elleanthus lentii*) which has nearly completed its molt. Its new tenth primary is already in place, while the ninth is still growing.

Molt is also involved in attaining adult plumage. The Violet Sabrewing **above left**, feeding at a poró (*Erythrina gibbosa*), is molting into adult male plumage, exchanging dull green feathers for violet. Most young hummingbirds are duller versions of the adults, often with buff fringes to the feathers covering their upperparts. Full adult plumage is attained within a few weeks of fledging.

Apart from hermits, which are relatively sedentary, most Costa Rican hummingbirds move to new areas when they finish breeding. Patterns of movement are complex, with some species moving to higher altitudes while others are moving down. Yet others spread out in all directions.

In the Monteverde area, for example, most hummers finish breeding around April. Individuals of many species move down the Caribbean slope while other individuals remain behind—there is simply a shift in the center of abundance of the population to lower altitudes. April and May are also the months when rare or vagrant hummingbirds turn up in the Monteverde community. A few Brown Violet-ears arrive from the Caribbean slope every year, along with the odd White-necked Jacobin and Green Thorntail. Plain-capped Starthroats arrive from lower down the Pacific slope, attracted by the flowering of the vine *Mandevilla veraguasensis* (page 118).

Two common species are present in Monteverde for only a few months of the year. The Magenta-throated Woodstar goes there to breed. Males arrive in September, a few weeks ahead of the females, and set up territories. Breeding finishes by the end of March and both sexes depart in April or May. Apart from an occasional young bird, Woodstars are absent from Monteverde for several months. Where they go in the nonbreeding season is unknown.

Unlike the Woodstar, the Scintillant Hummingbird is a nonbreeding visitor to Monteverde. Scintillant Hummers breed on the Pacific slope of the central volcanoes and Talamancas. They spread out after the breeding season, moving northwest along the central divide, as well as up and down the mountain slopes. Some birds reach Monteverde and remain from about March until June.

Above a Magenta-throated Woodstar at a bromeliad, *Tillandsia insignis*; **above right** a Brown Violet-ear at *Clusia stenophylla*; and **below right** a Scintillant Hummingbird at *Palicourea lasiorrhachis*.

The changing climate has affected numerous birds and other animals in Costa Rica. Hummingbirds are no exception, and the ranges of many are shifting upward. In the 1980s, Fiery-throated Hummingbirds were common in the higher parts of the Monteverde Preserve, particularly along the Chomogo and Brillante Trails. Now they are scarce. Rich patches of ericaceous flowers that used to be defended by Fiery-throated Hummingbirds have mostly been taken over by Purple-throated Mountaingems. Sadly, since the Cordillera de Tilarán is a low range, it seems likely that the Fiery-throat will be lost from the area before long.

There are other signs of change. We used never to see Steely-vented Hummingbirds around our house, even though they were always common only a short distance downhill. Now they are predictable postbreeding visitors every year in May and June. Again, Peter Feinsinger, referring to the area of the Monteverde community in the 1970s, wrote that Magenta-throated Woodstars "appeared predictably and abundantly from September through April." Now they are uncommon in Monteverde, although they are still fairly numerous higher up, near the Monteverde Preserve. During the 1980s, Purple-throated Mountaingems were the most numerous hummingbird at the feeders at the Hummingbird Gallery. Now they are far outnumbered by Green-crowned Brilliants.

Elsewhere in Costa Rica, at Savegre Lodge on the Cerro de la Muerte, Volcano Hummingbirds no longer outnumber Scintillant Hummingbirds at the feeders, as they did only a few years ago.

Above a Fiery-throated Hummingbird at *Heliconia monteverdensis*; and **right** a Steely-vented Hummingbird at *Stachytarpheta frantzii*.

THE HUMMINGBIRDS OF COSTA RICA

Hummingbirds originated in South America and spread north as Central America came into being, first as a chain of islands and then as a land bridge linking North and South America. Hummingbirds have continued to evolve in Central America, particularly in the isolated Costa Rica–Chiriquí highlands, which have long been a center of speciation and endemism.

More than half of Costa Rica's hummingbird species are widespread in Central and South America, many ranging from Mexico to Venezuela, Colombia, or Ecuador. Of the remainder, several species belong to what are, in effect, South American genera (including the White-tipped Sicklebill, Green-fronted Lancebill, Green Thorntail, and Green-crowned Brilliant) that reach their northern limit in Costa Rica. The Cinnamon Hummingbird belongs to the distinctive tropical dry forest avifauna that extends south from Mexico and reaches its southern limit in Guanacaste. The remaining species belong to the Costa Rica–Chiriquí faunal region. Nine species (ten including the distinctive southern race of the Magnificent Hummingbird) live only in the highlands. These include the endemic Coppery-headed Emerald, which occurs only in the northern and central cordilleras of Costa Rica, and the near-endemic Gray-tailed Mountaingem. In addition, the Beryl-crowned Hummingbird and White-crested Coquette have a limited range at low to mid-elevations in southwestern Costa Rica and adjoining Panama.

Of the forty-five hummingbirds that breed in Costa Rica, six are hermits that inhabit rainforest at low or mid-elevations. They barely enter the dry forest, with only the Green Hermit ranging as high as 2,000 m. The remaining thirty-nine typical hummingbirds are distributed between all Costa Rican habitats, including mangroves and páramo. Apart from the hermits, few hummingbirds dwell in the forest understory, and those that do so are mainly females. Most are found in forest canopy, treefall gaps, open woodland, scrubby pastures with scattered trees, and gardens.

The highest hummingbird diversity in Costa Rica is found in the foothills and wet mid-elevations of the Caribbean slope. At elevations between 100 and 1,000 m, the diversity does not vary much. Gary Stiles recorded twenty species at an altitude of 100 m at La Selva Biological Station (fourteen of them residents or regular visitors), and twenty-two species at an altitude of 1,000 m in Braulio Carrillo National Park (seventeen residents or regular visitors). Further north, we have recorded a similar number at 800 m on the Caribbean slope of the Cordillera de Tilarán (twenty-six species with sixteen residents or regular visitors). Fewer hummingbirds occur in the flat Caribbean lowlands away from the mountains or in the rather isolated Corcovado National Park.

Diversity decreases at higher altitudes. Above 1,500 m in the Monteverde Cloud Forest Preserve there are twelve hummers that are resident or regular visitors. Above 2,000 m on the Cerro de la Muerte, the number drops to five breeding species, and only the Volcano Hummingbird ranges above timberline (at about 3,000 m) into páramo. The Guanacaste dry forest (excluding gallery forest) has four resident species and several regular visitors, including the Ruby-throated Hummingbird, which is a common winter visitor from North America

At the present time, no Costa Rican hummingbird is in imminent danger of extinction. The majority are described in *A Guide to the Birds of Costa Rica* as abundant, common, or locally common. The eight hummingbirds that are rarer include such notable species as the White-tipped Sicklebill, Green-fronted Lancebill, Brown Violet-ear, both Coquettes, Green Thorntail, Snowcap, and Magenta-throated Woodstar. None of these is seriously threatened. All but the White-crested Coquette and Woodstar live in wet mid-elevation forests on the Caribbean slope, a habitat that is well represented in Costa Rica's excellent system of national parks and private reserves. The White-crested Coquette's stronghold is the Osa Peninsula, much of which is protected, and the El General valley, where it seems to survive quite well in a mosaic of forest patches, scrub, and agriculture. The Magenta-throated Woodstar was previously listed as near-threatened by Birdlife International, but has been reassessed and is not included in recent publications.

The endemic Mangrove Hummingbird is described as locally common in *A Guide to the Birds of Costa Rica* but is listed as endangered in Birdlife International's *Threatened Birds of the World* (2000). It remains locally common along the Pacific coast but merits its endangered status because it has a small, fragmented range and its specialized habitat is itself threatened. Its prospects have been improved recently by the establishment of the Térraba-Sierpe National Mangrove Forest Reserve, which protects the most extensive area of mangroves in the country. Other protected areas in which the Mangrove Hummingbird occurs include Curú National Wildlife Reserve, Tivives Mangrove Reserve, and Ballena National Marine Park.

Left a Green Hermit visiting a poró, *Erythrina gibbosa*.

The unmistakable Sicklebill is a foothill species that seldom strays far into flat lowland terrain. It occurs more or less along the whole length of the Caribbean slope and on the southern half of the Pacific slope. It is most abundant in the very wet zone between 300 and 800 m elevation, where it frequents the forest understory and lush second growth.

The Sicklebill visits only a limited selection of flowers. The most important are species of *Heliconia* with curved flowers, notably *pogonantha*, *longa*, *trichocarpa*, and, to a lesser extent, *reticulata*. It also visits the similarly curved flowers of *Centropogon granulosus*. One might expect that the Sicklebill's extraordinary bill would give it exclusive feeding rights at these flowers. Not so—it shares all of them with other hermits (pages 42, 44, and 77), including the relatively short-billed Barbthroat (page 75) and the Bronzy Hermit. The Sicklebill almost invariably perches to feed, though we have sometimes seen it hover at *Centropogon granulosus*. Like other hermits, it takes many spiders.

Male Sicklebills join small leks in dense *Heliconia* thickets, drawing attention to themselves with their spluttery song. Occasionally they sing singly.

Though uncommon and rarely encountered by chance, the Sicklebill is not too difficult to find, provided one makes the effort to watch appropriate flowers at dawn. La Selva Biological Station and Sirena (in Corcovado National Park) are good localities to try, while the Quebrada Gonzalez area of Braulio Carrillo National Park is even better.

A White-tipped Sicklebill perched **right** and at *Heliconia reticulata* **left**.

The Bronzy Hermit is superficially similar to the Band-tailed Barbthroat. Both lack the long central tail feathers of other hermits but boast striking tail patterns—rufous, black, and white in this species, black and white only in the Barbthroat. The sexes are similar.

This Hermit's range in Costa Rica is similar to that of the Barbthroat, differing only in being restricted to slightly lower elevations. It is found in forest margins, in clearings with dense thickets of *Heliconia*, and in overgrown banana plantations. It is a trapliner and feeds at much the same range of flowers as other hermits.

Male Bronzy Hermits are unusual among hermits in not forming leks. They are also unusual among hummingbirds in general in forming a lasting pair bond. Males are known to attend and guard the nest, mainly against other Bronzy Hermits, but play no role in building it, incubating the eggs, or feeding the young. There is also evidence of a relationship that is more than a brief encounter in the closely related Rufous-breasted or Hairy Hermit (which is sometimes lumped with the Bronzy Hermit). In Trinidad, males and females have been noted duetting—singing with alternating phrases.

We have encountered this species most frequently on the Osa Peninsula and at La Selva Biological Station, but it can be seen at most lowland rainforest sites.

Above a Bronzy Hermit at a passion flower, *Passiflora vitifolia*.

The Band-tailed Barbthroat is a typical hermit in its general appearance, but it is easily identified by its eye-catching tail. Like its relatives, it is often inquisitive, hovering at arm's length with tail spread, displaying its conspicuous pattern. The sexes are similar.

The Barbthroat is widely distributed in wet, forested areas of the Caribbean and south Pacific slopes, and ascends the adjoining mountain slopes to an altitude of about 600 m. It spends more time in the forest understory than most hummingbirds and is often seen in dense, lush thickets of *Heliconia* and similar broad-leaved herbs. It traplines scattered flowers and is a frequent visitor to shellflowers (*Calathea*), which it pierces, as well as to gingers (*Costus*) and *Heliconia*.

On the Pacific slope, at least, the Barbthroat is one of the few hummingbirds to have a significant song. Alexander Skutch described it as a "true songster," with a repertoire that includes plaintive trills and warbles. On the Caribbean slope, the song is shorter and more typical of hummingbirds generally. Males often form leks of two or three birds but also sing alone. As in the previous species, male Barbthroats sometimes attend nesting females.

The Band-tailed Barbthroat is easily seen at many lowland rainforest sites, including Tortuguero, Corcovado, and Carara National Parks. The successional plots at La Selva Biological Station are good, particularly those with abundant *Heliconia pogonantha*.

Above a Band-tailed Barbthroat at *Heliconia pogonantha*.

Recently, some authorities have split this species, with Costa Rican birds becoming the Western Long-tailed Hermit (*Phaethornis longirostris*). It is a bird of wet lowland forest on the Caribbean and south Pacific slopes and rarely ascends much above 600 m elevation. It is a classic high-reward trapliner and visits scattered flowers along regular routes up to a kilometer long. Even hermits occasionally enjoy a change, and we once watched a Long-tailed Hermit defending an exceptionally good patch of the passion flower *Passiflora vitifolia*.

The high-reward flowers visited by hermits are so constructed that pollen is brushed on to specific, different parts of a pollinator's body, which helps to prevent pollen from getting mixed. There is an interesting example of this in the Caribbean lowlands, where two closely related species of *Heliconia* (*umbrophila* and *irrasa*) bloom in the same small forest clearings at the same time. Both have long, curved flowers and are often visited in quick succession by Long-tailed Hermits. The flowers of *umbrophila* are curved downward **below left** and pollen is brushed onto the hermit's chin. But the flowers of *irrasa* are curved upward. To get its down-curved bill into these flowers, the hermit is forced to turn its head upside-down **above left**, thereby collecting pollen on its crown. In this photograph, the hermit has split the underside of the flower and its head is not in the correct position to contact the stamens. *H. trichocarpa* **right** grows in a different habitat and flowers at a different time of year.

Male Long-tailed Hermits join leks that may include well over twenty individuals. In Guyana, leks of the same species may comprise a hundred or more.

This species is abundant in lowland rainforest and is one of the easiest hummingbirds to see.

The sexes are similar in most hermits but differ in this species. The male is mainly dark green, while the female has gray underparts and buff stripes on its head.

The Green Hermit is widely distributed in wet mountain forests, from Costa Rica along the Andes to southern Peru. In Costa Rica, it is found on both slopes between about 700 and 2,000 m, though some, mainly young, birds move to lower altitudes outside the breeding season.

The Green Hermit traplines a great variety of flowers, including such common, showy species as gingers (*Costus*), members of the acanthus family (*Razisea spicata* and *Aphelandra tridentata*), and the bromeliad *Guzmania nicaraguensis*, all of which get fewer visits than might be expected given that they are clearly adapted to be pollinated by long-billed hummingbirds. Unlike its Costa Rican relatives, the Green Hermit often ascends high into the canopy to feed at epiphytes, such as gesneriads (*Columnea*) and bromeliads. Like other hermits, it also spends a lot of time gleaning spiders and insects from spiders' webs.

For much of the year, up to twenty males gather at traditional leks in dark forest understory, where they sit, tails bobbing, and call for long periods. Their "song" is a nasal, froglike note repeated about once a second—*ad infinitum*.

The Green Hermit is abundant and easy to see at all mid-elevation and cloud forest sites. It is an occasional visitor to the feeders at the Hummingbird Gallery in Monteverde and at Mirador Cinchona in the Sarapiquí Valley.

Male Green Hermits at a gesneriad, *Columnea purpurata* **above**, and a bromeliad, *Guzmania nicaraguensis* **below right**; and a female at *Razisea spicata* **above right**.

The Little Hermit is one of the smallest hummingbirds, weighing less than 3 g. Recently, some authorities have placed it in a separate genus from the larger hermits and split it into several species. The Costa Rican birds then become the Stripe-throated Hermit (*Phaethornis* or *Pygmornis striigularis*).

The Little Hermit is common on the Caribbean and south Pacific slopes up to about 1,200 m and in places even higher. Unlike other hermits, it also occurs, albeit in low numbers, in evergreen gallery forest in the Guanacaste lowlands. Though it does not stray far from forest, it is mostly seen in edge habitats and readily enters large clearings and gardens. It is a low-reward trapliner, visiting a great variety of scattered flowers, including many pollinated by insects. It often pierces flowers with long tubular corollas, such as *Heliconia mathiasiae* and the passion flower *Passiflora vitifolia*. It also takes advantage of holes made by bees.

Foraging birds often attract attention by the loud and rather distinctive buzz made by their wings.

Up to twenty-five males form leks in dense understory, where they utter their high-pitched, squeaky song from low perches, often only 20–30 cm above the ground.

The Little Hermit is common and easily seen at all lowland rainforest sites.

Left a Little Hermit at a ginger, *Renealmia cernua*, and **above** at a rattlesnake plant, *Calathea crotalifera*.

GREEN-FRONTED LANCEBILL

The Green-fronted Lancebill frequents wet mid-elevation forests, between about 800 and 2,200 m on the Caribbean slope but rarely below 1,500 m on the Pacific slope.

The Lancebill is a high-reward trapliner, though males sometimes defend large clumps of flowers against other Lancebills. Within its altitudinal range, it is the only hummingbird with a very long, straight bill. Green Hermits visit a few of the same flowers, but Lancebills have more or less exclusive use of any canopy species with a straight tubular corolla 30–40 mm long. They especially favor species with long pendant flowers, such as the epiphytic heaths *Psammisia ramiflora* and *Satyria warszewiczii*, and the mistletoe *Psittacanthus nodosus*. They also like the flowers of the tree *Symplocos povedae* and various bromeliads, mainly species of *Guzmania*.

Lancebills are frequently seen perched by mountain streams, often choosing a pool below a waterfall, where they hawk low over the water for insects. In the Monteverde Cloud Forest Preserve, the pool below "La Catarata" on the Río Trail is a good place to look for them, especially at dawn and in the late afternoon.

The Lancebill is one of the less common Costa Rican hummingbirds, but streams at Tapantí, Savegre, and Wilson Botanic Garden are suitable places to search for them. We have also had good success by finding and watching the right canopy flowers.

Left and **right** a Green-fronted Lancebill at an epiphytic heath, *Psammisia ramiflora*.

The Scaly-breasted Hummingbird is rather similar in size, structure, and behavior to a Sabrewing, and nowadays it is sometimes included in the genus *Campylopterus*, instead of in the monotypic *Phaeochroa*. The sexes are alike and rather nondescript, but their large size, and the white corners to the tail, makes them fairly easy to identify.

The Scaly-breasted Hummingbird is widely distributed on the Pacific slope, up to an altitude of about 1,200 m in the southwest. It also occurs in the Río Frío area south of Lake Nicaragua, but is rare everywhere else on the Caribbean slope. It occurs mostly in forest edge and semi-open areas, and in mangroves in Guanacaste. Though sometimes territorial, it more often behaves as a marauder. Favorite flowers include those of various trees such as *Inga* and *Erythrina*, several species of *Heliconia*, *Pelliciera* when in mangroves, and the terrestrial bromeliad *Bromelia pinguin* in Guanacaste.

Male Scaly-breasted Hummingbirds form loose leks of usually fewer than a dozen individuals. Their song is loud and, for a hummingbird, quite musical.

Though not always present, the Scaly-breasted Hummingbird is usually easy to find at Wilson Botanic Garden, where there is an active lek for much of the year. Curú, Carara, and the mangroves at the mouth of the Río Tárcoles are also dependable areas.

Left and **above** a Scaly-breasted Hummingbird at *Heliconia latispatha*.

The Violet Sabrewing is one of the biggest hummingbirds, similar in size to the Sicklebills, Crimson Topaz, Great Sapphirewing, and Sword-billed Hummingbird, and is clearly surpassed only by the much bigger Giant Hummingbird. It is widespread in the mountains of Costa Rica, mostly between 1,500 and 2,200 m, with many birds moving to lower elevations after breeding. It seems to reach Carara National Park quite regularly.

The Sabrewing resembles the hermits in having a longish curved bill and in being a high-reward trapliner. It keeps fairly low in the forest, visiting many of the same flowers as hermits, including gingers (*Costus*), gesneriads (*Columnea*, *Drymonia*), and several members of the Acanthaceae (*Razisea spicata*, *Justicia aurea*, and *Aphelandra*). It also favors *Heliconia* and is a frequent visitor to banana plantations. Around our house in Monteverde, Sabrewings trapline the bat-pollinated bromeliad *Vriesia nephrolepis* at dawn to feed

on leftover nectar. A few individuals also visit the plants at dusk to pierce and extract nectar from buds that are about to open. Sabrewings are rarely territorial at flowers, though they easily dominate all other Costa Rican hummingbirds at feeders.

Males sometimes sing singly, but normally join small leks of four to six birds in forest undergrowth.

The Violet Sabrewing is easy to see at most cloud forest sites. It is a very common visitor to feeders at the Hummingbird Gallery in Monteverde, and at La Paz Waterfall Garden and Mirador Cinchona in the Sarapiquí valley.

Male Violet Sabrewings **above left** at *Heliconia monteverdensis*, **below left** at a gesneriad, *Columnea glabra*, and **above** at a ginger, *Costus montanus*; and a female **right** at *Ravnia triflora*.

The White-necked Jacobin has an enormous range from southern Mexico through Central America to Bolivia and the Amazon basin. In Costa Rica it occurs mainly below 500 m along the entire length of the Caribbean slope and on the southern Pacific slope. It ranges widely after breeding, many individuals moving to higher altitudes, at least temporarily.

The male Jacobin is boldly patterned and one of the most unmistakable hummingbirds. A few females are unusual in resembling males, distinguishable only by their slightly smaller size, but typical females are much duller and a little reminiscent of a female Green-crowned Brilliant. Both sexes adopt a characteristic posture when hovering at flowers.

The Jacobin is mainly a canopy species. Like the Brown Violet-ear, it is strongly attracted to *Inga* and to the small, globular, berrylike flowers of the cerillo tree *Symphonia globulifera*. It also enters clearings and light gaps to feed in thickets of *Heliconia latispatha* and at rubiaceous shrubs such as *Hamelia* and *Palicourea*.

Jacobins spend more time catching tiny flies than almost any other hummingbird we know. We have often seen them in long, sustained maneuvers above the canopy or in a break above a forest stream. They are supremely elegant in flight, twisting and turning, and fanning their tail in an intricate ballet that is a delight to see.

Although widespread and not uncommon, the Jacobin is prone to disappear from some areas for months at a time and is not always easy to find. The hummingbird feeders at Villa Borinquen, near Ujarráz in the Sarapiquí valley, are a reliable site for much of the year. Otherwise, the Sarapiquí lowlands and the Osa Peninsula are the best areas to look.

Above a female White-necked Jacobin at *Heliconia latispatha*; and **right** a male at a bromeliad, *Guzmania lingulata*.

The aptly named Brown Violet-ear has unusual coloration for a hummingbird. Though nowhere common, it has an extensive range, from Mexico through Colombia and the Guianas to Bolivia and eastern Brazil. In Costa Rica, it breeds mainly at mid-elevations on the Caribbean slope, but wanders widely afterward.

The Brown Violet-ear is mainly a canopy species, foraging at flowering trees (*Symphonia*, *Inga*, and *Calliandra*) and epiphytes (*Clusia* and *Norantea*), many of which are usually pollinated by insects. It rarely defends a territory but, when it does so, easily holds its own against Rufous-tailed Hummingbirds and other habitual territorialists. It is also opportunistic. Two individuals of this species took advantage of an exceptional display of more than 160 flowering spikes of the orchid *Elleanthus glaucophyllus* that appeared on a log near our house. This hummingbird-pollinated orchid normally occurs in clumps of only a few flowering spikes and

is typically visited by low-reward trapliners such as female Purple-throated Mountaingems and Coppery-headed Emeralds.

During the breeding season, males sing in small leks. A nest has never been found in Costa Rica.

The Brown Violet-ear is uncommon. It is easiest to see after the breeding season, when it disperses to both lower and higher elevations. From late April to June, or later, it is a regular visitor to feeders at La Paz Waterfall Garden and Mirador Cinchona in the Sarapiquí valley. During the same months, small numbers appear in the Monteverde area and often visit the feeders at the Hummingbird Gallery.

Brown Violet-ears at *Norantea costaricensis* **left** and an epiphytic orchid, *Elleanthus glaucophyllus* **above**.

The Green Violet-ear is a beautiful bird with peacock-blue iridescence and a glorious tail that is often fanned. The violet "ears" are flared in display (page 16). The sexes are almost alike.

The Green Violet-ear is an abundant highland species, occurring from as low as 1,400 m in the Cordillera de Tilarán up to 3,000 m in the Talamancas. It is an altitudinal migrant, moving to lower altitudes after breeding. In the Monteverde area, most of the population leaves for a few weeks from July until the end of August.

Unlike the Brown Violet-ear, this species is a bird of forest edge, clearings, and even pastures with scattered large trees. Sometimes it defends a territory, but where it lives alongside the more dominant Fiery-throated Hummingbird and Mountaingems, it spends more time traplining scattered flowers. This habit ensures that it feeds at and pollinates many different flowers. Favorites include mints (*Salvia*), epiphytic heaths (*Cavendishia*, *Gonocalyx*, and *Macleania*), and the smaller species of *Centropogon* and *Bomarea*. It often hawks tiny insects from a perch, like a flycatcher.

Males form small gatherings in which they keep well apart but close enough to hear each other. They tirelessly repeat their metallic chips and chirrups from a high exposed twig, carrying on for most of the day for seven or eight months of the year.

The Green Violet-ear is easy to see. It is a common visitor to feeders at highland sites, including Monteverde, the Sarapiquí valley, and Cerro de la Muerte.

Green Violet-ears at an epiphytic orchid, *Elleanthus glaucophyllus* **above**, and two epiphytic heaths, *Gonocalyx costaricensis* **above right** and *Cavendishia capitulata* **below right**.

The Green-breasted Mango ranges from Mexico to Peru. Some specialists split the Central American populations into two species, with birds from Costa Rica and further north called Prevost's Mango, and Panamanian birds Veraguas Mango. The latter, which lacks black on the throat, occurs just across the border with Panama and is quite likely to turn up in southwestern Costa Rica. The male Mango is easily identified, while the female, with its black breast stripe and chestnut tail, is even more distinctive. Young birds (see also page 24) resemble females except for a chestnut stripe on their sides.

As a species of open country and savannas, the Mango used to be confined to the Pacific slope north of the Río Tárcoles, and to the Río Frío area just south of Lake Nicaragua. Forest clearance has enabled it to extend its range southward on the Pacific slope to Dominical, and on the Caribbean slope to Guápiles and beyond. It is found mainly below 300 m elevation, though we have seen stragglers at altitudes up to 800 m on the Caribbean slope of the Cordillera de Tilarán, and to 1,500 m on the Pacific slope.

Typical hummingbird flowers are relatively scarce in the Guanacaste dry forest, where the Green-breasted Mango is most frequent. There, like other dry forest hummingbirds, Mangos depend heavily on trees, particularly legumes, whose massed flowers are pollinated by bees and other insects. They also favor the spectacular but transitory abundance of flowers provided by "big bang" trees such as corteza (*Tabebuia ochracea*) and *T. impetiginosa*. On the Caribbean slope, the choice of flowers is much greater and Mangos visit a wide variety of typical hummingbird flowers, as well as canopy trees. Wherever it occurs, the Mango spends much time hawking for insects.

Above a male Green-breasted Mango at *Heliconia latispatha*; **above right** a female at *Tabebuia impetiginosa*; and **below right** a young bird at a bromeliad, *Guzmania lingulata*.

The male Violet-headed Hummingbird is distinctive, but the rather nondescript female (page 62) is very similar to the females of several other species. The conspicuous white spot behind the eye is a good identification aid for both sexes.

The Violet-headed Hummer is common below about 1,000 m on the Caribbean and south Pacific slopes. It moves lower after breeding but seldom ventures away from the foothills. It frequents the canopy, second growth, and clearings and readily enters gardens close to forest.

Though very small and low in the hummingbird pecking-order, males set up territories if they can find enough flowers that are free. They defend them fiercely against other small hummers, as well as bees, wasps, and butterflies. Females forage as low-reward trapliners and filchers, often stealing nectar in the territories of Crowned Woodnymphs. Flowers favored by both sexes include *Inga*, *Hamelia*, and *Stachytarpheta*.

Males form small leks, usually in rather open, sunny woodland, and defend perches about 8–10 m above the ground. The song is the usual small hummingbird medley of tuneless, high-pitched chirps and squeaks. The female almost invariably builds her tiny nest on a small twig or liana overhanging a forest stream and decorates it beautifully with strands of moss.

The Violet-headed Hummer is common at many rainforest sites, particularly in the foothills of the Caribbean slope. Any patch of *Stachytarpheta* in the vicinity of forest is almost bound to attract a few.

Above a Violet-headed Hummingbird at *Hamelia patens*.

The White-crested Coquette, also known as the Adorable Coquette, is . . . adorable. To add to its charm, it can be extremely confiding, allowing approach to within almost touching distance. The ornate male is unmistakable, but the female may be confused with the female Black-crested Coquette. The white throat is the best distinguishing character. Stiles and Skutch suggest that males may go into eclipse after breeding, based on the paucity of males in full regalia seen between April and August.

The White-crested Coquette is confined to the south Pacific slope of Costa Rica and a small area of adjacent Panama. It is a canopy species, feeding primarily at insect-pollinated flowers of trees, including *Inga*, mayo (*Vochysia*), and cashews (*Anacardium*). It also visits clearings and gardens to feed at *Stachytarpheta* and other small flowers.

A courting male White-crested Coquette is said to hover in front of the female, moving from side to side in short arcs. We have never seen this display, but the description is reminiscent of close-encounter displays of several other tiny hummingbirds.

We know of no reliable site to see this elusive species, but possibilities are the El General valley, including Alexander Skutch's farm "Los Cusingos," and the lodges on the Osa Peninsula and around Golfito.

Above right and **right** a male White-crested Coquette at a flowering cashew, *Anacardium occidentale.* Note that its white crest is only half-grown.

The Black-crested Coquette was formerly known as Princess Helena's Coquette, no doubt in honor of some European noblewoman whose family members were patrons of scientific collecting. It is a scarce bird in Costa Rica, found only on the Caribbean slope, mainly between 300 and 1,000 m.

Like other Coquettes, it is mainly a canopy species, feeding at trees such as *Inga*, *Dipteryx*, and mayo (*Vochysia*), but descends into clearings to feed at *Stachytarpheta* and a variety of small, insect-pollinated flowers. As well as a trapliner, it is a persistent filcher, slipping away from irate territorialists only to return quietly within seconds. With its conspicuous white rump and insectlike flight, it bears a striking resemblance to several species of white-rumped hawkmoths (*Aellopus*) that can often be seen hovering at the same flowers. Territorial hummers, particularly the larger ones, often do not bother to chase off insects, so Coquettes may derive some advantage from the resemblance.

Black-crested Coquettes can be very tame. The male seen here continued to feed while we watched from a distance of less than half a meter.

Though widespread on the Caribbean slope, it is nowhere common. The most reliable site we know of is Villa Borinquen, near Ujarráz in the Sarapiquí valley, where Coquettes enter the garden to feed at *Stachytarpheta*.

A male Black-crested Coquette **above**; and a male **above right** and female **below right** feeding at *Stachytarpheta frantzii.*

This attractive and distinctive species is at its northern limit in the Cordillera de Tilarán, and ranges as far south as Ecuador. In Costa Rica, it is confined to the very wet mid-elevations of the Caribbean slope, between about 800 and 1,400 m.

The Green Thorntail is essentially a canopy species. It feeds at the flowers of many trees and epiphytes, but seems particularly attracted to *Inga*, *Quararibea costaricensis*, and *Clusia*. Like Coquettes, it also visits clearings and gardens to feed at *Stachytarpheta*. In the early wet season, after breeding, it descends to lower altitudes, sometimes reaching the Sarapiquí lowlands and La Selva Biological Station, where it is almost always seen at the colorful rubiaceous tree *Warszewiczia coccinea*. When hovering, it has the same characteristic posture as many other tiny hummers, with the tail cocked at almost a right angle. In the male, because of its long tail, the posture appears even more exaggerated.

The Thorntail used to be difficult to see at close quarters, but has become a reliable visitor to the feeders at La Paz Waterfall Garden and Mirador Cinchona in the Sarapiquí valley. The male seen here was perched on twigs just a few meters from the viewing balcony at Mirador Cinchona.

A male Green Thorntail perched **above**; and females perched **left** and feeding at *Stachytarpheta frantzii* **right**.

FORK-TAILED EMERALD

There are several closely related populations of small Emeralds ranging from northwestern Mexico through Central America to northern South America. They have been variously treated as a single species—the Blue-tailed Emerald (*Chlorostilbon mellisugus*)—or as many as eight. Nowadays, the Mexican and Central American populations are sometimes split into five or six species. As far as Costa Rica birds are concerned, two are often accepted. Birds from the northern part of the Pacific slope are then called Salvin's Emerald (*C. salvini*), while birds from southwestern Costa Rica, which have a black bill and a less forked tail, are called Garden Emerald (*C. assimilis*). However, Stiles and Skutch give reasons for continuing to classify all Costa Rican birds as a single species.

The Fork-tailed Emerald (or Salvin's Emerald) is widespread on the Pacific slope, below about 1,500 m, where it frequents forest edge, cleared scrubby areas, and gardens. It is a tiny species and a classic low-reward trapliner and filcher.

Popular flowers include *Hamelia*, *Lobelia laxiflora*, *Stachytarpheta*, and many insect flowers. It also pierces flowers such as sleeping hibiscus (*Malvaviscus arboreus*).

This species is generally common within its range, particularly in the foothills. We have found it easy to see around the Monteverde community, while the Garden Emerald is frequently seen at Wilson Botanic Garden.

Male Fork-tailed Emeralds at *Stachytarpheta frantzii* **above** and a gesneriad, *Kohleria spicata* **above right**; and a male Garden Emerald **below right**.

Nowadays most authorities call this species the Purple-crowned or Violet-crowned Woodnymph. With its glittering violet and green plumage and forked tail, the unmistakable male is among the loveliest hummingbirds. The female, though dull and unremarkable, can be distinguished from other female hummingbirds by its contrasting gray and greenish underparts.

The Crowned Woodnymph is not found in the dry-forested northern Pacific slope, but is common elsewhere in wet, forested country throughout the lowlands and foothills of Costa Rica, up to about 800 m. For much of the year, males forage in the canopy, at epiphytic heaths, bromeliads, gesneriads (*Columnea*), and at other epiphytes. Females spend more time in the forest understory, where they feed at a variety of rubiaceous shrubs, including *Hamelia*, *Palicourea*, and hotlips (*Cephaelis*). They also favor the huge terrestrial bromeliad *Bromelia magdalenae*. After the breeding season, which ends in June, many birds of both sexes are heavily dependent on *Heliconia* species with short flowers, particularly *H. latispatha*. Some move upward to mid-elevation forests, where they often join other hummingbirds at flowering *Inga* trees. Males are aggressive and defend territories at major flower concentrations.

The Crowned Woodnymph can easily be seen at all major lowland rainforest sites, including La Selva Biological Station and Braulio Carrillo, Tortuguero, Corcovado, and Carara National Parks.

Male Crowned Woodnymphs alighting on *Heliconia latispatha* **left** and **above right**; and a male molting into adult plumage at a gesneriad, *Columnea linearis* **below right**.

The Fiery-throated Hummingbird is confined to the Costa Rica–Chiriquí highlands, where it inhabits oak forests between 1,500 and 2,000 m.

It is a stunningly beautiful bird, provided it is seen in good light, from in front and slightly above. Otherwise it looks just blackish or dull, glossy green. Though the male is distinctly larger, both sexes are brightly colored and both defend a territory. Fiery-throats are aggressive territorialists and dominate even mountaingems in areas where they overlap. They usually set up territories in the forest canopy, especially at epiphytic heaths (*Cavendishia* and *Satyria*), but they also descend to lower levels to feed at small trees, shrubs, *Heliconia*, and other herbs. They readily pierce flowers with long corolla tubes and also take advantage of holes made by Slaty Flowerpiercers and bees.

Fiery-throats are unusual among hummingbirds in that a sort of pair bond is formed during the breeding season. The belligerence of the males enables them to defend more flowers than they need themselves, leaving a surplus for the use of females.

The Fiery-throat is one of a number of Costa Rican hummingbirds that are being affected by global warming. It has become scarce in most of the area that it formerly occupied in the Monteverde Cloud Forest Preserve and persists there only on the highest peaks and ridges. Clumps of epiphytic heaths, formerly defended by Fiery-throats, are now "owned" by Purple-throated Mountaingems.

The Fiery-throated Hummer is easily seen around the summits of Poás and Irazú volcanoes, and in the Talamancas. It is a common visitor to the feeders at La Georgina on Cerro de la Muerte.

Fiery-throated Hummingbirds at *Fuchsia splendens* **above**, *Fuchsia microphylla* **above right**, and a bromeliad, *Vriesia ororiensis* **below right**.

This species is sometimes called the Blue-throated Sapphire to conform with the names given to the South American members of the genus. With its glittering gorget and lustrous tail, the male Blue-throated Goldentail is spectacular. The female is similar but duller, the blue gorget being reduced to blue spotting. The red on its bill is also less extensive.

The Golden-tail occurs over much of Costa Rica, up to about 800 m. It is a bird of light secondary growth, overgrown clearings, and forest margins. In arid Guanacaste, it prefers gallery forest. Both sexes trapline flowers and rarely defend territories.

For eight or nine months of the year, males gather in small leks of three to ten birds, perched on bare twigs, 8–10 m above the ground. Their loud and cheerful song draws attention to the leks. Males sing less when the weather is very dry or very wet.

Golden-tails are relatively scarce on the Caribbean slope but often abundant in the south Pacific lowlands and foothills, including the Osa Peninsula. The easiest way to see them is probably to locate assemblies of singing males.

A female Blue-throated Goldentail perched **right** and at *Stachytarpheta frantzii* **above**.

In most books and checklists this species is known as the Charming Hummingbird. It has a very small range, being confined to the south Pacific slope and adjacent Panama, up to altitudes of about 1,200 m. It is closely related to the Blue-chested Hummingbird of the Caribbean slope, the two species replacing each other geographically on opposite sides of the Talamancas. They are often considered to be the same species.

Like most of its relatives, the Beryl-crowned Hummer occurs in forest edge, open woodland, and treefall gaps. It is often found in coffee plantations, particularly those in which the shade trees are *Inga*. Both sexes are attracted by a wide range of flowers, including *Inga*, rubiaceous shrubs (*Cephaelis*, *Hamelia*, and *Palicourea*) and *Heliconia*. In the higher parts of its range, above 1,000 m, it also feeds at epiphytic heaths such as *Satyria*.

The Beryl-crowned Hummer is common in most suitable habitat and is easily found along the Pacific coast from Carara southward, in the El General valley, on the Osa Peninsula, and at Wilson Botanic Garden.

Above a male Beryl-crowned Hummingbird perched on an epiphytic heath, *Satyria warszewiczii*, at the center of its territory.

This species is called the Lovely Hummingbird in some old books, and nowadays it is sometimes put in the genus *Polyerata* instead of *Amazilia*. It has an extensive range from Nicaragua to western Ecuador. In Costa Rica, it is confined to the humid lowlands and foothills of the Caribbean slope, rarely rising above 300 m. It is replaced in similar habitat on the south Pacific slope by the closely related Beryl-crowned Hummer.

The Blue-chested Hummingbird is a bird of second growth, old clearings, and river banks, as well as overgrown plantations and shady gardens. Preferred flowers include those of several trees, notably *Inga* and *Warszewiczia*, and rubiaceous shrubs such as *Hamelia* and *Palicourea*. The Blue-chested Hummer is a would-be territorialist but is almost invariably thwarted by one or another of several dominant species that share the same habitat, including the Rufous-tailed Hummingbird, Crowned Woodnymph, and Red-footed Plumeleteer.

The Blue-chested Hummer is one of the many species in which males gather in small leks and sing with great persistence for much of the year.

It is easily found in suitable habitat, including Tortuguero and Cahuita National Parks. It is almost always to be found at dawn at clumps of *Hamelia patens* growing around the laboratories and accommodation at La Selva Biological Station.

Above a male Blue-chested Hummingbird at *Hamelia patens*.

The Mangrove Hummingbird is sometimes put in the genus *Polyerata* instead of *Amazilia*. The male is easily identified by its sharply demarcated green and white underparts. It could only be confused with the Snowy-bellied Hummingbird, but that is a foothill species and the ranges of the two do not overlap. The rather nondescript female resembles several other female hummingbirds. She is green above and pale below, much like the female Beryl-crowned Hummingbird, and the two occur in fairly close proximity in some coastal areas south of the Río Tárcoles.

The Mangrove Hummingbird is one of two hummers that are endemic to Costa Rica. It is found from the shores of the Golfo de Nicoya south along the Pacific coast to the Osa Peninsula, including the Golfo Dulce. It is listed as endangered by Birdlife International because its total range is small and fragmented, and because its specialized habitat is threatened by illegal cutting and the construction of salt pans and shrimp ponds.

As its name suggests, the Mangrove Hummer is more or less confined to mangroves, where it especially favors the large white blossoms of the Pacific mangrove (*Pelliciera rhizophorae*). Though it never strays far, the Mangrove Hummer readily flies a few hundred meters inland to join other hummingbirds at flowering trees.

The Mangrove Hummingbird can be seen fairly easily at many sites where mangroves are accessible, including Curú, Tivives, Tárcoles, Uvita, the mouth of the Río Grande de Térraba, and Puerto Jiménez. We have found it easiest to find, and have had better views of it, however, at flowering trees in the vicinity of mangroves. At Rancho La Ensenada in the dry season, for example, any flowering *Inga* or *Tabebuia* seems to attract two or three Mangrove Hummers.

Male Mangrove Hummingbirds at *Tabebuia impetiginosa* **above** and *Inga vera* **above right**; and a female at *Inga vera* **below right**.

The Steely-vented Hummingbird is sometimes put in the genus *Saucerottia* instead of *Amazilia*. The isolated northern population (formerly *sophiae*, now *hoffmanni*), which is found in Nicaragua and northwestern Costa Rica, is sometimes considered distinct from South American birds, and is then known as the Blue-vented Hummingbird (*Amazilia* or *Saucerottia hoffmanni*). In Costa Rica, it is found on the Pacific slope north of Carara National Park, ranging up to about 1,500 m. In the Monteverde area, at least, some birds cross the continental divide and move to mid-elevations on the Caribbean slope around May and June, when *Inga oerstediana* is flowering. We have seen a few individuals at the same time of year in the Sarapiquí valley on the Caribbean slope of Volcán Poás.

Male and female Steely-vented Hummers are alike, and both defend territories. They are the dominant territorialist at mid-elevations, but subordinate to the slightly larger Cinnamon Hummingbird where they overlap in lowland Guanacaste. They frequent scrubby woodland, coffee plantations, and gardens, foraging at many flowering trees, including *Pithecellobium*, *Inga*, and *Tabebuia*, as well as at shrubs and herbs (*Hamelia*, *Stachytarpheta* and *Lobelia*).

The Steely-vented Hummingbird is abundant, particularly in the foothills, and easily seen throughout northwestern Costa Rica. It is common around the Monteverde community, though not higher up near the cloud forest.

Above a male Steely-vented Hummingbird at *Stachytarpheta frantzii*.

The Snowy-bellied Hummingbird is sometimes put in the genus *Saucerottia* instead of *Amazilia*. The male and female are alike and resemble the male Mangrove Hummingbird in having a shiny green breast that contrasts sharply with a white belly. There is little chance of confusion, however, because this is a foothill species, found mainly between 300 and 1,600 m elevation, which does not occur close to mangroves.

The Snowy-bellied Hummer has a fairly limited range in southwestern Costa Rica, including the El General valley but excluding the much wetter areas around the Golfo Dulce. It inhabits open woodland, coffee plantations, and gardens, where it visits the flowers of many shrubs and herbs, including *Palicourea*, *Hamelia*, and *Stachytarpheta*. It also forages high up in the canopy of flowering trees such as mayo (*Vochysia*), *Inga*, and *Calliandra*. In Wilson Botanic Garden, it is a regular visitor to an Australian bottlebrush tree (*Callistemon violaceum*) that grows outside the dining room.

Unlike many of the other hummers alongside which it lives, the male Snowy-bellied Hummer sings solitarily and inconspicuously. It seems never to join singing assemblies.

Two of the best places to see this species are the El General valley, including Alexander Skutch's farm "Los Cusingos," and Wilson Botanic Garden.

Above a Snowy-bellied Hummingbird at *Hamelia patens*.

The Cinnamon Hummingbird is an inhabitant of the dry forest region that stretches south from Mexico along the Pacific coast, reaching its southern limit in Guanacaste. It is a member of the characteristic avifauna endemic to the region, which also includes the Lesser Ground-Cuckoo, Elegant Trogon, Magpie Jay, and Banded Wren, among others.

In Costa Rica, the Cinnamon Hummer ranges as far south as Tárcoles and upward into the foothills of the northern cordilleras to altitudes of about 500 m. It goes higher, to about 1,000 m, on the approaches to the Valle Central.

With its distinctive coloring, it is an easily identified species. The sexes are similar, apart from the male having more red on its bill, and both are aggressive territorialists. Like other dry forest hummers, Cinnamon Hummingbirds spend most of the dry season foraging at trees whose main pollinators are bees and other insects. They are attracted to legumes, such as *Inga* and *Caesalpinia*, and to the synchronized "big bang" flower displays of species of *Tabebuia*. In the wet season flowers are scarcer. The big terrestrial bromeliad *Bromelia pinguin*, which forms dense stands in parts of the dry forest, is important for a while when it flowers around April or May. Other useful flowers include the introduced flamboyant tree (*Delonix regia*), a native of Madagascar, which is widely planted around towns and houses. It flowers in May and June and attracts a few hummingbirds as well as many butterflies.

The Cinnamon Hummer is one of the easiest hummingbirds to see, particularly in the dry season. It is abundant in all the Guanacaste parks and reserves and occurs in most hotel gardens.

Above a male Cinnamon Hummingbird at *Inga vera* (the pink blossom in the background is *Cassia grandis*).

The Rufous-tailed Hummingbird ranges from Mexico to Ecuador. It is the most widespread hummer in Costa Rica and a familiar sight in gardens, even in the center of San Jose. It is absent from mountains above about 1,800 m and is scarce in the dry-forested northwest. It prefers relatively open country, large clearings with scattered trees, riverbanks, and gardens and often finds its way to isolated clearings, even when they are surrounded by extensive forest on all sides.

The sexes are fairly similar in the Rufous-tail, although the female (page 63) has a less extensive glittering green breast and less red on the bill. Both sexes are aggressive and dominant over most other hummers with which they come in contact. Males commonly defend territories at clumps of *Hamelia*, *Heliconia*, and other popular flowers. We have also often seen them feed at flowers more typically visited by hermits, such as the introduced *Passiflora coccinea* and even the long, strongly curved flowers of *Heliconia stilesii*.

Males typically sing on their territory but sometimes join loose singing assemblies in areas where flowers are scarce. Nests are usually in fairly exposed sites and can often be found in hotel gardens.

The Rufous-tail cannot be missed and is likely to be the first hummingbird seen on any visit to Costa Rica.

Above a male Rufous-tailed Hummingbird at *Heliconia latispatha*.

The Striped-tailed Hummingbird frequents wet, mid-elevation forests the length of the country but, unlike most Costa Rican hummers, is curiously patchy in its distribution. Some birds descend to lower elevations after breeding.

Male Striped-tails occur mainly in the forest canopy, while females dwell more in the forest understory. Both sexes pierce flowers, including buds that are about to open, with great regularity, more so than any hummer except the Purple-crowned Fairy, which is a lowland species. Striped-tails are particularly attracted to *Razisea spicata*, *Justicia aurea*, and other members of the Acanthaceae, whose papery-thin flowers are easy to pierce. Striped-tails also visit many other flowers in the conventional way, particularly *Inga*, *Quararibea* and other trees, epiphytes such as *Clusia* and *Norantea*, and numerous shrubs and herbs.

As well as feeding in the forest understory, females also build their nests there (page 62). All the ones we have seen

were in deep forest, low down, and usually close to a stream. All were decorated with long, dangling strands of moss.

Though quite difficult to find in much of its Costa Rican range, the Striped-tailed Hummingbird is common and easily seen in the Monteverde Cloud Forest Preserve and is a frequent visitor to feeders at the Hummingbird Gallery.

Male Striped-tailed Hummingbirds about to pierce flowers of the vine *Mandevilla veraguasensis* **above left**; piercing *Aphelandra tridentata* **below left** and *Justicia aurea* **right**; and feeding legitimately at *Hansteinia blepharorhachis* **above**.

The Black-bellied Hummingbird is endemic to the Costa Rica–Chiriquí highlands. It occurs on the Caribbean slope from the Cordillera Central southward along the Talamancas at altitudes between 1,200 and 2,000 m.

Though related to the Striped-tailed Hummingbird, and having similar rufous secondaries, the Black-bellied Hummer is more like a Coppery-headed Emerald in size and behavior. The two species overlap only on the north slope of the Cordillera Central, where the Coppery-headed Emerald occupies a slightly lower range of altitudes. Male Black-bellies spend much time in the canopy and defend patches of epiphytic heaths (*Cavendishia*) or other good flowers whenever they have the opportunity. Females spend more time in the understory and gaps, where they visit *Palicourea*, *Besleria*, *Gonzalagunia*, and numerous other small flowers. Both sexes feed at flowering trees such as *Inga* and *Pithecellobium*.

The Black-bellied Hummingbird is common in Braulio Carrillo and Tapantí National Parks though, being a canopy species, it is not always easy to see well. It is, however, a reliable visitor to the feeders at La Paz Waterfall Garden.

Above a male Black-bellied Hummingbird feeding at a gesneriad, *Kohleria spicata*.

The White-tailed Emerald is yet another hummingbird that is confined to the Costa Rica–Chiriquí highlands. It is closely related to the Coppery-headed Emerald, replacing it in southern Costa Rica and western Panama. The male differs in lacking any sign of coppery tints on its crown and rump, and both sexes have a straight, rather than slightly decurved, bill. In spite of its name, the White-tailed Emerald has less white in its tail than either the Coppery-headed Emerald or the Black-bellied Hummingbird. However, it occupies a different range, within which it is the only small hummer with mainly white outer tail feathers.

In Costa Rica, the White-tailed Emerald is confined to the Pacific slope of the Talamancas and the southern coastal ranges and it is most numerous between 800 and 1,400 m. It is very similar to the Coppery-headed Emerald in its feeding behavior. Males forage mainly in the forest canopy, visiting a variety of trees (*Symphonia*, *Inga*, *Quararibea*) and epiphytes (*Cavendishia*, *Clusia*), while females spend more time in the forest understory. Both sexes visit coffee plantations, clearings, and gardens to feed at *Palicourea*, *Stachytarpheta*, and other shrubs.

The White-tailed Emerald is seasonally common in and around Wilson Botanic Garden near Las Cruces.

Above a female White-tailed Emerald at *Hamelia patens*.

COPPERY-HEADED EMERALD

The Coppery-headed Emerald is endemic to Costa Rica, where it is confined to the northern cordilleras and the Cordillera Central. The male is easily identified by its coppery crown and rump and flashing white tail feathers. The tail pattern also distinguishes the female, except on the slopes of the Cordillera Central, where the female Black-bellied Hummer has an overlapping range and a rather similar tail pattern. The latter has rufous secondaries and grayer underparts.

The Coppery-headed Emerald frequents wet mountain forests and edges, breeding between 800 and 1,600 m but descending as low as 300 m on the Caribbean slope after breeding. Males forage mainly in the canopy, at trees such as *Inga* and *Quararibea*, and at many epiphytes, including epiphytic heaths (*Cavendishia*), *Clusia*, and orchids (*Maxillaria*, *Elleanthus*). Females spend more time in the forest understory, where they visit *Besleria*, *Palicourea*, and other small flowers. Both sexes visit clearings and gardens.

Males sing and display in small groups, frequently indulging in aerial chases. The female usually builds her nest in the forest understory, occasionally in the open. The nest is similar to those of the Violet-headed and Striped-tailed Hummingbirds (page 62).

This is a common cloud forest species and easily seen at hummingbird feeders in Monteverde and the Sarapiquí valley.

Male Coppery-headed Emeralds at *Palicourea padifolia* **above**, an epiphytic orchid, *Maxillaria fulgens* **above right**, and *Symphonia globulifera* **below right**.

The Snowcap is tiny. Weighing only 2.5 g, it is about the same size as a Volcano Hummer and smaller than a Coquette. With its shining white cap and unique maroon-purple plumage, the exquisite male is unlike any other hummer. The female, on the other hand, resembles several other small female hummers and has no very obvious distinguishing marks.

The Snowcap is a Central American species that ranges from Honduras to western Panama. In Costa Rica, it breeds at lower mid-elevations the length of the Caribbean slope, between 300 and 700 m, but is most frequently encountered on the slopes of the Cordillera Central. After breeding, a few individuals move up temporarily to 1,000 m or so, but most descend to the foothills, with some reaching the Sarapiquí lowlands. This is a canopy species, feeding at trees such as *Inga*, *Pithecellobium*, and *Warszewiczia coccinea* but descending to shrub level at edges and in clearings.

The Snowcap is not an easy hummingbird to see except at Rancho Naturalista, near Turrialba, where it visits hummingbird feeders. It is quite common in the lower parts of Braulio Carrillo National Park and occurs regularly at La Selva Biological Station in May and June, where it is almost invariably seen at *Warszewiczia*, *Hamelia*, or *Stachytarpheta*.

Above a male Snowcap feeding at the tiny flowers of the tree *Warszewiczia coccinea* (the bright red "petals" are actually sepals).

With its streamlined shape and clean-cut colors, the Purple-crowned Fairy is arguably the most elegant and graceful of Costa Rican hummingbirds. The sexes are rather similar, the male being distinguished most easily by its violet forehead and crown.

The Fairy is widespread in forested areas on the Caribbean slope, from the lowlands up to about 1,200 m. On the south Pacific slope it occurs as far north as Carara. It frequents the forest canopy, treefall gaps, and flowery gardens. It is usually seen singly.

The Fairy's habits are less refined than its appearance, for it is an inveterate thief. It uses its short needlelike bill to extract nectar through the back of otherwise inaccessible, long, or large flowers. It easily punctures the tough waxy flowers of poró species (*Erythrina*) and *Heliconia mathiasiae*, but also steals from an enormous variety of blooms, large and small. It even robs the 10-cm-long flowers of *Posqueria*

latifolia, a species pollinated by long-tongued hawkmoths, and the large blue blossoms of the introduced Asian sky vine (*Thunbergia grandiflora*). The Fairy is more insectivorous than most hummingbirds, spending much time gleaning from foliage and hawking midges in gaps in the canopy.

The Fairy is neither particularly common nor predictable at any given site, but one or two are likely to be seen most days in suitable habitat. We have the impression that it is most frequent in the lower mid-elevations on both slopes, between 300 and 800 m.

Above a female Purple-crowned Fairy at *Heliconia mathiasiae*.

This species goes by the name of Bronze-tailed Plumeleteer in most books and checklists, but it is an inappropriate name for the Costa Rican members of the species, since their tail is not bronze. Red-footed Plumeleteer is more apt and distinctive, particularly in view of the rarity of red feet among hummingbirds.

In Costa Rica, the Red-footed Plumeleteer is confined to forested regions on the Caribbean slope, ascending to about 700 m in the foothills. It frequents forest edge, old second growth, and treefall gaps but seldom strays far from good forest. It is a very aggressive, dominant species. Males are territorialists, controlling prime patches of such flowers as *Hamelia patens*, hotlips (*Cephaelis*), and species of *Heliconia* with short flowers (including *latispatha*, *imbricata*, and *sarapiquensis*). Females seldom defend territories but, being large and aggressive, often forage as marauders.

The Red-footed Plumeleteer is widespread in the lowlands, occurring in Tortuguero and Cahuita National Parks, but it seems most numerous in the Sarapiquí lowlands, especially at La Selva Biological Station, where it is common. Compared with most hummingbirds it is rather shy, which can give a false impression of its status. When its voice is known, a truer picture emerges.

Male Red-footed Plumeleteers at *Heliconia sarapiquensis* **left** and *Hamelia patens* **above**.

The White-bellied Mountaingem is endemic to the Costa Rica–Chiriquí highlands. Within Costa Rica, it is confined to a rather narrow altitudinal zone in the very wet mid-elevations of the Caribbean slope, from Volcán Arenal southward. On the slopes of the Cordillera de Tilarán, for example, it is common only between 1,000 and 1,300 m.

Within this narrow zone, males are the dominant territorialist. Like other Mountaingems, they frequent the canopy, treefall gaps, and clearings, where they defend high-quality patches of epiphytic heaths (*Cavendishia*, *Satyria*, and *Thibaudia*) and rubiaceous shrubs such as *Palicourea* and hotlips (*Cephaelis*). They are virtually certain to be found feeding at any flowering *Quararibea costaricensis*. The smaller females tend to be low-reward trapliners, visiting scattered flowers, including bromeliads (*Guzmania*), gesneriads (*Columnea*), and butterfly-pollinated species such as the balsam *Impatiens walleriana* and the milkweed *Asclepias curassavica*.

The White-bellied Mountaingem is common in its preferred altitudinal zone and can be found easily on the Caribbean slope of the Cordillera de Tilarán, in the Peñas Blancas and San Gerardo valleys, and in Braulio Carrillo National Park. However, it is easiest to see in the Sarapiquí valley, where it is a common visitor to the feeders at Mirador Cinchona (although it is uncommon higher up the valley at La Paz Waterfall Garden).

Above a male White-bellied Mountaingem.

The Gray-tailed Mountaingem is virtually endemic to the Cordillera de Talamanca, being replaced abruptly at the Panama border by the closely related White-throated Mountaingem. The two forms, which differ only in tail color, are lumped together by some authorities. In the past, both were lumped with Purple-throated birds, the whole complex then being known as the Variable Mountaingem (*Lampornis castaneoventris*). The females of both the Gray-tailed and White-throated forms are almost identical to the female Purple-throated Mountaingem (pages 18, 21, 46, and 130).

The Gray-tailed species inhabits oak forest from about 1,800 m up to timberline. Like the Purple-throated Mountaingem, the male is the dominant hummingbird in the lower parts of its range, but subordinate to the Fiery-throated Hummer at higher altitudes. Males defend high-quality flowers in the canopy where they can, especially clumps of epiphytic heaths (*Cavendishia* and *Satyria*), but make do with flowering shrubs, including *Centropogon* and *Fuchsia*, where necessary.

The Gray-tailed Mountaingem is fairly common on Cerro de la Muerte. It can be reliably seen at Savegre Lodge, where it is a regular visitor to the feeders.

Above a male Gray-tailed Mountaingem.

The Purple-throated Mountaingem is very common in cloud forest in the northern Cordilleras and the Cordillera Central, its center of abundance being between 1,500 and 2,500 m. It is absent from most of the Talamancas, where it is replaced by the closely related Gray-tailed Mountaingem.

Male Purple-throated Mountaingems are very aggressive. In the lower parts of their range, they are the dominant territorialist, defending the best patches of epiphytic heaths (*Cavendishia*, *Macleania*, and *Satyria*). Though they stay mainly in the canopy, they readily descend into treefall gaps and clearings to feed at flowering rubiaceous shrubs, notably *Cephaelis*, *Palicourea*, and *Gonzalagunia*. At higher altitudes, where they overlap, they are subordinate to the bigger and even more aggressive Fiery-throated Hummingbird. Female mountaingems are much smaller than the males and forage by traplining scattered or low-quality flowers, including many that are pollinated by insects.

As in other mountaingems, the males sing on their territories to attract females. The quiet but attractive song is a prolonged medley of splutters, trills, and musical warbles.

The Purple-throated Mountaingem is easy to see at a number of sites, including the Monteverde Cloud Forest Preserve and the Braulio Carrillo and Tapantí National Parks. It is a frequent visitor to the feeders at the Hummingbird Gallery in Monteverde and La Paz Waterfall Garden.

Purple-throated Mountaingems visiting two species of epiphytic heaths—a male at *Macleania insignis* **above** and a female at *Cavendishia melastomoides* **left**.

The Green-crowned Brilliant is sometimes more aptly known as the Green-fronted Brilliant. The spectacular male has a distinctive long, deeply forked tail. Its plumage often resembles shiny plated armor, gleaming from all angles, and its upright stance enhances a rather military look. The female (see also pages 15 and 32), with its green-spangled underparts, is easily identified. Young birds of both sexes, with cinnamon throat and cheeks, seem to cause identification problems for visiting birders and are the reason for many sightings of hummingbirds that are "not in the book."

The Brilliant is common throughout the wet, forested highlands of Costa Rica at altitudes between 800 and 2,000 m. Two or three competing males are often seen chasing each other in towering ascents, high above the forest canopy, while females are frequent in the forest understory, hawking for insects from a low perch. Both sexes visit many typical hummingbird flowers, including *Heliconia*, *Costus*,

Drymonia, and numerous bromeliads. They have strong feet and usually perch to feed.

Brilliants spend more time than most hummingbirds feeding on left-over nectar at bat-pollinated flowers, including bromeliads *Vriesia*, the vine *Mucuna urens*, and the strange inflorescences of *Marcgravia*. In some areas, the breeding season of Brilliants is even timed to coincide with the flowering of *Marcgravia* species, rather than with typical hummingbird flowers.

The Green-crowned Brilliant is easily encountered at highland sites such as Monteverde, Tapantí, and Guayabo. It is abundant at feeders at the Hummingbird Gallery in Monteverde, La Paz Waterfall Garden, and Mirador Cinchona.

Male Green-crowned Brilliants at *Heliconia tortuosa* **above left** and at a bromeliad, *Pitcairnia brittoniana* **above**; an immature male at a ginger, *Costus montanus* **below left**; and a female at a gentian, *Symbolanthus pulcherrimus* **right**.

The Magnificent Hummingbirds found in Costa Rica and western Panama, which are bigger than those that range from the United States to Nicaragua, are sometimes regarded as a separate species called the Admirable Hummingbird (*Eugenes spectabilis*). As such, it belongs to the select group of species that are endemic to the Costa Rica–Chiriquí highlands.

The Magnificent Hummer is common in the oak forests of the Cordillera Central and Cordillera de Talamanca at elevations above 2,000 m. It is a large, long-billed hummingbird and fills the trapliner niche at high altitudes, where no hermits occur. The female has a longer bill than the male and traplines more (page 45). In fact, males are often territorial, particularly during the breeding season, when they defend large patches of giant thistles (*Cirsium*). Other flowers favored by both sexes include the larger species of climbing lilies (*Bomarea*), *Fuchsia splendens* (one of the sources of cultivated *Fuchsia* varieties), a gentian (*Symbolanthus pulcherrimus*), and the long-flowered, rose-lavender species of *Centropogon* (*C. gutierrezii* on Volcán Poás and Volcán Irazú, and *C. talamancensis* in the Talamancas).

The Magnificent Hummer is easily seen on Poás and Irazú Volcanoes and along the road that crosses Cerro de la Muerte. In the latter area, it is a common visitor to the feeders at both Savegre Mountain Lodge and La Georgina.

Left male Magnificent Hummingbirds; and **right** a male on a giant thistle, *Cirsium subcoriaceum*, at the center of its territory.

The Plain-capped and Long-billed Starthroats are closely related and very similar in appearance. They replace each other in different parts of Costa Rica, the former occupying the drier northwest and central valley, the latter the rest of the country. The two species overlap somewhat in the El General-Térraba region, although the Long-billed Starthroat is much more common there.

Both are birds of the canopy, forest edge, banana and coffee plantations, and open country with scattered trees. Both are very fond of the long bladelike flowers of several species of poró (*Erythrina*), and they often defend them against other Starthroats. In the northwest the Plain-capped Starthroat feeds at many of the same flowers as other dry forest hummers, notably *Tabebuia*, *Ceiba*, *Bombacopsis*, and the introduced flamboyant tree (*Delonix regia*). The Long-billed Starthroat favors *Heliconia mathiasiae* and other species of *Heliconia* with long straight flowers, as well as the flowers of cultivated bananas. Both Starthroats spend much time catching small insects, usually in prolonged darting flights high above the treetops.

Unusual for hummingbirds, Starthroats habitually rest, roost, and nest on exposed bare branches, where they lack any protection from inclement weather.

The best way to find Starthroats is to watch flowering *Erythrina* trees or scan high, exposed branches in suitable habitat. In Monteverde, the entrance to the Bajo del Tigre trail is a good area for the Plain-capped Starthroat. There, in the wet season, it is a regular visitor to the flowers of the vine *Mandevilla veraguasensis* (page 118).

A Long-billed Starthroat perched **left** and at a poró, *Erythrina gibbosa* **above**.

The Magenta-throated Woodstar occurs on the Pacific slope of Costa Rica and western Panama, mostly between 1,000 and 1,600 m. It frequents semi-open areas and forest margins, but also forages in the forest canopy. Though generally rare, it is sometimes locally common, as at Monteverde, where it arrives to breed in October and stays until about May. Apart from an occasional young bird, it is absent from June until September. Where it goes is unknown. A few have been seen at mid-elevations on the Caribbean slope in May and June, soon after their departure from Monteverde.

Woodstars feed at numerous different flowers, including *Inga*, *Quararibea*, and many epiphytes. They are aggressive and territorial among themselves, but often forage as filchers. When hovering, they have a characteristic appearance, with cocked tail, like the Coquettes and Thorntail. Their flight is smooth and beelike, accompanied by the loudest hum of any Costa Rican hummingbird.

Males have an impressive display flight in which they swoop back and forth over a female or intruding male, each dive being accompanied by a snipelike bleating noise, followed by manakin-like snaps. Presumably the sound effects are made by the wings. Males also have a pleasant spluttering, warbling song. Females have twice nested close to our house, high up on exposed twigs (and at least twice on a television aerial in Monteverde).

The Woodstar is easy to see in Monteverde from October to May, especially at feeders at the Hummingbird Gallery. It also visits the feeders at La Paz Waterfall Garden during the same months.

Right a male Magenta-throated Woodstar at an epiphytic heath, *Cavendishia complectens*; and **above** a female at *Lobelia laxiflora*.

The Scintillant Hummingbird is Costa Rica's smallest bird. It breeds at mid- to high elevations on the Pacific slope from the Cordillera Central south to Chiriquí in Panama. It frequents brushy areas, overgrown pastures, and hedgerows, where it feeds mainly at insect-pollinated flowers.

After breeding, Scintillant Hummingbirds disperse, moving to higher altitudes on the central volcanoes as well as northwest along the Cordillera de Tilarán. Small numbers reach Monteverde by the beginning of March, sometimes earlier, and most depart in June. Six or seven inhabit the shrubby fields around our house, feeding at flowers of *Clusia, Gonzalagunia*, and *Rubus* and filching in the territories of Purple-throated Mountaingems, Green Violetears, and Coppery-headed Emeralds.

Breeding males greet females and intruders with dive displays. In lieu of a song, their outer flight feathers make a characteristic metallic whistling sound when they fly.

The Scintillant Hummer is probably easiest to see at Savegre Mountain Lodge on Cerro de la Muerte, where it is a regular visitor to the feeders. In fact, it appears to be getting more numerous there, while the Volcano Hummingbird is getting scarcer. This is probably a consequence of the changing climate.

Above a male Scintillant Hummingbird at *Gonzalagunia rosea*; **above right** a female at an orchid, *Elleanthus glaucophyllus*; and **below right** a young bird at an insect-pollinated epiphytic heath, *Vaccinium poasanum*. Young birds resemble females but have rusty fringes on the upperparts.

Populations of Volcano Hummingbirds on different mountains have different colored gorgets—rose-red on Volcán Poás and Volcán Barva, purple on Volcán Irazú, and a rather dull, purplish-gray in the Talamancas. The population on Poás and Barva was formerly regarded as a separate species, the Cerise-throated Hummingbird (*Selasphorus simoni*). The female of all forms resembles the female Scintillant Hummingbird, but is whiter below, less buffy, with more conspicuous white tips to the outer tail feathers.

Volcano Hummingbirds are common in the Cordillera Central and Cordillera de Talamanca, from about 2,000 m up to the top of the highest peaks.

Both sexes are mainly low-reward trapliners and filchers. They visit many different flowers, including some favored by Fiery-throated Hummingbirds (*Fuchsia microphylla* and *F. paniculata*), as well as insect-pollinated flowers such as *Ocotea* and the mistletoe *Gaiadendron punctatum*.

Breeding males defend territories that are often on the summit of small hills or hummocks. The male has a spectacular display in which it rises vertically up over its territory before hurtling back down, calling and snapping its wings.

The Volcano Hummingbird is very easy to see in suitable habitat on Volcán Poás, Volcán Irazú, and Cerro de la Muerte. It is a common visitor to the feeders at Savegre Mountain Lodge and La Georgina.

Above a female Volcano Hummingbird at the mint *Salvia iodochroa*; and **right** Talamanca males at a climbing lily, *Bomarea hirsuta*.

HUMMINGBIRD SITE GUIDE

It has never been easier to see a good selection of hummingbirds in Costa Rica. The proliferation of hummingbird feeders at tourist facilities guarantees superb views of about half of Costa Rica's hummingbirds, including such spectacular species as Violet Sabrewing, Fiery-throated Hummingbird, Green Thorntail, Snowcap, and Magenta-throated Woodstar. Our choice of the birding areas and sites listed here is highly selective. Most are places that we know well ourselves, but a few have been included because they are visited by many birders. We have also mentioned several establishments with popular well-kept hummingbird feeders. There are doubtless others that we have not had the opportunity to visit.

The site guide covers all forty-five hummingbird species that breed in Costa Rica and also the Ruby-throat. Species are included in the site lists **only** if they are seen regularly at appropriate times of year.

GU   Guanacaste. Includes Santa Rosa and Palo Verde National Parks, Lomas Barbudal Biological Reserve, Rancho La Ensenada, and the Nicoya beaches. Most Guanacaste hummingbirds are common and can be seen in any well-wooded area, at least in the dry season.

MV   Monteverde. Includes the hotel areas as well as the Monteverde Cloud Forest Preserve, Children's Rainforest, and Santa Elena Reserve. The altitudinal range is from about 1,300 m in Santa Elena and Monteverde on the Pacific slope to above 1,600 m along the continental divide and down to about 800 m on the Caribbean slope. Hummingbirds found only in the Peñas Blancas and San Gerardo valleys on the Caribbean slope are marked "C." There are good hummingbird feeders at the Hummingbird Gallery close to the entrance to the Monteverde Cloud Forest Preserve.

PS   Poás–Sarapiquí. Volcán Poás National Park and a transect from Varablanca down the upper Sarapiquí valley as far as Virgen del Socorro. The altitudinal range is from 2,700 m on Volcán Poás down to 1,700 m at Varablanca and 800 m at Virgen del Socorro. Hummingbirds found only in Volcán Poás National Park and the higher parts of the transect are marked "H." There are feeders at La Paz Waterfall Garden and Mirador Cinchona. There are also feeders at Villa Borinquen, a few kilometers below Virgen del Socorro, just past Ujarráz.

BC   Braulio Carrillo National Park adjacent to the highway, including the trails at Quebrada Gonzales but not including the higher elevations of Volcán Barva. The altitudinal range is from about 2,000 m close to the Zurqui Tunnel down to 500 m at Quebrada Gonzales.

TA   Tapantí National Park (1,300 m). The original area approached through Cartago and Orosi. The extensions up the Cerro de la Muerte are not included.

RN   Rancho Naturalista (1,000 m). There are feeders at the Lodge.

LS   La Selva Biological Station. The gardens around the laboratories, accommodations, and dining room are excellent in the early morning.

CC   The Caribbean coast, particularly Tortuguero and Cahuita National Parks.

CM   Cerro de la Muerte above about 2,000 m. There are hummingbird feeders at Savegre Lodge (2,200 m) and La Georgina (3,100 m).

WB   Wilson Botanic Garden (1,000 m). Includes the forest down to and across the Río Jaba. The Hummingbird and Heliconia Gardens are particularly good.

CA   Carara National Park and the adjoining coastal area around Tárcoles.

OS   The Osa Peninsula and protected areas around the eastern shores of the Golfo Dulce, including Golfito.

	GU	MV	PS	BC	TA	RN	LS	CC	CM	WB	CA	OS
White-tipped Sicklebill		C		x		x	x					x
Bronzy Hermit						x	x				x	x
Band-tailed Barbthroat				x			x	x		x	x	x
Long-tailed Hermit							x	x			x	x
Green Hermit		x	x	x	x	x				x		
Little Hermit	x	C	x	x		x	x	x		x	x	x
Green-fronted Lancebill		x	x	x	x					x		
Scaly-breasted Hummingbird	x									x	x	x
Violet Sabrewing		x	x	x	x				x	x	x	
White-necked Jacobin		C	x	x		x	x	x				x
Brown Violetear		x	x	x		x						
Green Violetear		x	x	x	x				x			
Green-breasted Mango	x						x				x	
Violet-headed Hummingbird		C	x	x		x	x	x		x		x
White-crested Coquette											x	x
Black-crested Coquette		C	x	x		x						
Green Thorntail		C	x	x		x						
Fork-tailed Emerald	x	x								x	x	x
Crowned Woodnymph		C	x	x		x	x	x		x	x	x
Fiery-throated Hummingbird		x	H						x			
Blue-throated Goldentail	x	x		x			x				x	x
Beryl-crowned Hummingbird										x	x	x
Blue-chested Hummingbird							x	x				
Mangrove Hummingbird	x										x	x
Steely-vented Hummingbird	x	x									x	
Snowy-bellied Hummingbird										x		
Cinnamon Hummingbird	x											
Rufous-tailed Hummingbird	x	x	x	x	x	x	x	x		x	x	x
Stripe-tailed Hummingbird		x										
Black-bellied Hummingbird			x	x	x							
White-tailed Emerald										x		
Coppery-headed Emerald		x	x	x	x							
Snowcap				x		x	x					
Red-footed Plumeleteer						x	x	x				
White-bellied Mountaingem		C	x	x	x							
Purple-throated Mountaingem		x	H	x	x							
Gray-tailed Mountaingem									x			
Green-crowned Brilliant		x	x	x	x	x			x			
Magnificent Hummingbird			H						x			
Purple-crowned Fairy		C	x	x		x	x	x		x	x	x
Plain-capped Starthroat	x	x										
Long-billed Starthroat							x			x	x	x
Magenta-throated Woodstar		x	x	x	x							
Ruby-throated Hummingbird	x											
Scintillant Hummingbird		x	H	x					x			
Volcano Hummingbird			H						x			

INDEX OF HUMMINGBIRD PHOTOGRAPHS

A Fiery-throated Hummingbird.

A Green Violet-ear at a mistletoe, *Psittacanthus ramiflorus.*

INDEX OF FLOWER PHOTOGRAPHS

SCIENTIFIC NAMES OF HUMMINGBIRDS

COMMON NAME (ENGLISH)	COMMON NAME (SPANISH)	SCIENTIFIC NAME
White-tipped Sicklebill	Pico de Hoz	*Eutoxeres aquila*
Bronzy Hermit	Ermitaño Bronceado	*Glaucis aenea*
Band-tailed Barbthroat	Ermitaño Barbudo	*Threnetes ruckeri*
Long-tailed Hermit	Ermitaño Colilargo	*Phaethornis superciliosus*
Green Hermit	Ermitaño Verde	*Phaethornis guy*
Little Hermit	Ermitaño Enano	*Phaethornis longuemareus*
Green-fronted Lancebill	Pico de Lanza Frentiverde	*Doryfera ludoviciae*
Scaly-breasted Hummingbird	Colibrí Pechiescamado	*Phaeochroa cuvierii*
Violet Sabrewing	Ala de Sable Violáceo	*Campylopterus hemileucurus*
White-necked Jacobin	Jacobino Nuquiblanco	*Florisuga mellivora*
Brown Violet-ear	Colibrí Orejivioláceo Pardo	*Colibri delphinae*
Green Violet-ear	Colibrí Orejivioláceo Verde	*Colibri thalassinus*
Green-breasted Mango	Manguito Pechiverde	*Anthracothorax prevostii*
Violet-headed Hummingbird	Colibrí Cabeciazul	*Klais guimeti*
White-crested Coquette	Coqueta Crestiblanca	*Lophornis adorabilis*
Black-crested Coquette	Coqueta Crestinegra	*Lophornis helenae*
Green Thorntail	Colicerda Verde	*Discosura conversii*
Fork-tailed Emerald	Esmeralda Rabihorcada	*Chlorostilbon canivetii*
Crowned Woodnymph	Ninfa Coronivioleta	*Thalurania colombica*
Fiery-throated Hummingbird	Colibrí Garganta de Fuego	*Panterpe insignis*
Blue-throated Goldentail	Colibrí Colidorado	*Hylocharis eliciae*
Beryl-crowned Hummingbird	Amazalia Corona de Berilo	*Amazilia decora*
Blue-chested Hummingbird	Amazalia Pechiazul	*Amazilia amabilis*
Mangrove Hummingbird	Amazalia Manglera	*Amazilia boucardi*
Steely-vented Hummingbird	Amazalia Culiazul	*Amazilia saucerrottei*
Snowy-bellied Hummingbird	Amazalia Vientriblanca	*Amazilia edward*
Cinnamon Hummingbird	Amazalia Canela	*Amazilia rutila*
Rufous-tailed Hummingbird	Amazalia Rabirrufa	*Amazilia tzacatl*
Striped-tailed Hummingbird	Colibrí Colirrayado	*Eupherusa eximia*
Black-bellied Hummingbird	Colibrí Pechinegro	*Eupherusa nigriventris*
White-tailed Emerald	Esmeralda Coliblanca	*Elvira chionura*
Coppery-headed Emerald	Esmeralda de Coronilla Cobriza	*Elvira cupreiceps*
Snowcap	Copete de Nieve	*Microchera albocoronata*
Red-footed Plumeleteer	Colibrí Patirrojo	*Chalybura urochrysia*
White-bellied Mountaingem	Colibrí Montañés Vientriblanco	*Lampornis hemileucus*
Purple-throated Mountaingem	Colibrí Montañés Gorgimorado	*Lampornis calolaema*
Gray-tailed Mountaingem	Colibrí Montañés Coligrís	*Lampornis cinereicauda*

COMMON NAME (ENGLISH)	COMMON NAME (SPANISH)	SCIENTIFIC NAME
Green-crowned Brilliant	Brillante Frentiverde	*Heliodoxa jacula*
Magnificent Hummingbird	Colibrí Magnífico	*Eugenes fulgens*
Purple-crowned Fairy	Colibrí Picopunzón	*Heliothryx barroti*
Plain-capped Starthroat	Colibrí Pochotero	*Heliomaster constantii*
Long-billed Starthroat	Colibrí Piquilargo	*Heliomaster longirostris*
Magenta-throated Woodstar	Estrellita Gorgimorada	*Calliphlox bryantae*
Scintillant Hummingbird	Chispita Gorginaranja	*Selasphorus scintilla*
Volcano Hummingbird	Chispita Volcanera	*Selasphorus flammula*

FURTHER READING

Numerous books about hummingbirds are available and more appear every year. We have found the following to be the most useful and best illustrated.

Burton, R. 2001. *The World of the Hummingbird*. Firefly Books, Willowdale, Ontario.
(A good up-to-date, popular account of the biology of hummingbirds. Includes photographs of many species.)

Del Hoyo, J., Elliot, A. and Sargantal, J. (eds). 1999. *Handbook of Birds of the World*, Volume 5. Lynx Edicions, Barcelona.
(The most comprehensive treatment of the hummingbirds of the world.)

Gould, J. A. 1849–1861. *Monograph of the Trochilidae, or Family of Hummingbirds*. Taylor and Francis, London. Reprinted 1990 as *Hummingbirds*. Wordsworth Editions, Ware, Hertfordshire.
(Includes sumptuous paintings of most species.)

Greenewalt, C. H. 1960. *Hummingbirds*. Doubleday & Company, Garden City, New York. Reprinted 1990. Dover Publications, New York.
(A general account including detailed descriptions of feather structure, iridescence, and flight. Includes photographs of many species.)

Mazariegos H., L. A. 2000. Hummingbirds of Colombia. Published by the author, Cali, Colombia.
(Deals with Colombian habitats, hummingbird biology, and conservation issues. Includes many beautiful photographs.)

Skutch, A. F. 1973. *The Life of the Hummingbird*. Vineyard Books, New York.
(A general account of the life of hummingbirds, written in the author's inimitable style.)

Stiles, F. G. and Skutch, A. F. 1989. *A Guide to the Birds of Costa Rica*. Cornell University Press, Ithaca, New York.
(Contains accounts and illustrations of all the hummingbirds recorded in Costa Rica.)

A male Green-breasted Mango perched on *Heliconia latispatha.*